th

Written in a conversational, accessible style and from a Christian faith perspective, *Life After Death: Practical Help for the Widowed* catalogues the experience of many widows and widowers at various stages along the way. These anecdotes and stories help newly grieving spouses know they are not alone and they are not crazy—two essential concepts for healing. Many people will find themselves within these pages, and come away with hope that they, too, will one day smile again.

—Amy Florian, MPS, FT
liturgy and bereavement consultant, and CEO of Corgenius

In *Life After Death: Practical Help for the Widowed*, Elizabeth Barkley tells the story of her journey into the unknown world of becoming a widowed person. Through self-disclosure—both hers and that of other widowed persons—plus excellent insights into the mourning process, she serves as a symbol of hope in helping bereaved persons accept the challenge of choosing life after death.

—Ken Czillinger
grief educator and cofounder of Parents of Murdered Children

This book is a gold mine filled with nuggets of practical suggestions from working with Social Security to buying a car. Barkley doesn't stop there— she takes one to a deeper level through her reflections, prayers, and role models at the end of each chapter. This book is truly a gift of inspiration, practicality, and spirituality.

—Jacqueline Leech, S.C.
chaplain, Gardens at St. Elizabeth, Denver, Colorado

Life After Death

practical help
for the
widowed

ELIZABETH BOOKSER BARKLEY, PH.D.

Franciscan
MEDIA
Cincinnati, Ohio

Cover design by Kathleen Lynch | Black Kat Design
Cover image © Punchstock | Digital Vision
Book design by Mark Sullivan

LIBRARY OF CONGRESS CATALOGING-IN-PUBLICATION DATA
Barkley, Elizabeth Bookser.
Life after death : practical help for the widowed / Elizabeth Bookser Barkley, Ph.D.
pages cm
Includes bibliographical references.
ISBN 978-1-61636-522-6 (alk. paper)
1. Bereavement—Religious aspects—Christianity. 2. Spouses—Death. 3. Widows—Religious life.
4. Consolation. I. Title.
BV4908.B37 2013
248.8'66—dc23
2012045378

ISBN 978-1-61636-522-6

Published by Franciscan Media
28 W. Liberty St.
Cincinnati, OH 45202
www.FranciscanMedia.org

Printed in the United States of America.
Printed on acid-free paper.
13 14 15 16 17   5 4 3 2 1

For my father, Wally,
whose life validates my belief
that one great love
does not preclude another.

CONTENTS

After my husband died, there was so much I wanted, wished, and hoped for. What else was there to do? His sudden, unexpected, and total absence left a space where, it seemed, only wanting, wishing, and hope could dwell.

Most of all, I just wanted to see.

He was fifty years old when he dropped off the treadmill that morning, leaving all of us behind. Leaving me, his children, stepchildren, parents, sisters, so many friends behind, he ran on.

For days, weeks, and months after the afternoon on which I got that unthinkable, disorienting phone call, it seemed as if all I was doing was straining to see.

I hadn't been there when he died, and it felt wrong and even unjust that this was the case. As awful as it sounds, I wanted to have been at the gym with him, I wanted to see, to see him alive one more time, even for those last seconds, instead of being left with the vision of his still body under harsh hospital lights.

I wanted to see him again, to see him now, to see where he was, to see that he was all right, and maybe even—as my faith taught me—more than all right. Better. The best, perhaps?

I wanted to see my boys'—his sons'—futures. They were four and seven when their father died, and if anything caused me to seize up in fear and anger it was the simple fact of them having to grow through childhood to manhood, through joy and suffering of all kinds, without their father's wisdom, humor, good sense, and support. I wanted to see far, far into the future and know that it would be all right. I wanted to see how it would come to that—what I was supposed to do to make it all right, to help them flourish and be secure in the strong love of a Father.

Mostly, I wanted to see the truth of it all. A serious Christian, a hopeful one, Mike's death shook me and shook my faith. What seemed not too challenging and an interesting subject for theological argument in the abstract, now became difficult: to see beyond the cold heavy flesh in the casket, so very present right there in the shadows of the funeral home—to light. I ached to see light, to see him safely in the light that would one day welcome us as well.

And I wanted to see, not only eternity, but today and tomorrow in the way that I had become used to, in the way that we had seen it together. For years, I had seen it all with him. We had seen it together. We didn't always see it the same way at all, but we understood—for me, grudgingly at times—the wholeness that was only possible because of the complementary vision of the other. With Mike, I could see. Life made sense.

Now it didn't. I so very much wanted it to. I wanted to see.

Now, I knew it was possible. Being a woman close to fifty myself, I'd known my share of death, dying, and those who had survived its presence close at hand. Widows, widowers, parents, children, friends—a world of men, women and children who had been touched by death and not only survived but seemed to flourish. They had not just "moved on," but they had moved through, grown wiser. They had not only not lost hope, they had grown in hope. They could say "Alleluia" at Easter— and mean it.

It was possible, then. But the way to that place was uncertain, at best. The destination was real. It existed. Others actually arrived there. They could see, it seemed. But how?

> "What do you want me to do for you?" He replied, "Lord, please let me see" (Luke 18:41).

Elizabeth Barkley is a wise, understanding guide for this journey. *Life After Death: Practical Help for the Widowed* is grounded in her own experience of widowhood, but embraces the experiences of others and pertinent research into the process of grieving.

Through her graceful and compassionate writing, Barkley generously offers wise companionship—the kind of companionship the widowed need: understanding and non-judgmental. There are no timetables or checklists, no right or wrong ways to grieve and then move on, she makes clear. But at the same time, what frames this wonderful book is the shared gift of a firm, yet gentle faith, vivid and hopeful because it has been lived and shared.

As Barkley points out throughout her book, this journey is a mixture—just like the rest of life—of choice and grace. We take steps, choosing to move forward, backwards or even in circles, and God meets us with grace. As Barkley says:

> With our choices come graces. God will not abandon us as we walk through this arid valley of death. So this book is also about graces we will encounter along the journey, if we stay open to them.

The blind man Bartimaeus took a step to Jesus and opened himself to the gift of presence. He moved, Jesus met him, he told Jesus what he sought, and he was healed. He could see.

—*Amy Welborn*

ACKNOWLEDGMENTS

For insights on grief: Ken Czillinger, James Ellis, Tim Harmon, Kathy McConnell, Janet McCord, Judy Sherlock.

For openness in sharing their grief journey: Wally Bookser, Beth Belknap Brann, Kathy Braswell, Linda Cardillo, Mary Kay Gilbert, Tom Hogan, Annie Horn, Liz Huesman, Cheryl Ilhardt, Barbara Kallmeyer, Tom Kanoza, Sherrin Knecht, Katie Lavelle, Dan Mader, Angie Meisman, Tim Meisman, Jane Phelan, Elaine Price, Richard Robbins, Judy Sherlock.

For invaluable feedback as my first readers: Andy Bockhold, Susan Brogden, Mary Kay Fleming.

For professional advice: Patrick Harmon, Mark Kleespies, Greg Luke, Peg Lynch, Kathy Owens, John Spaccarelli.

For publishing advice: Lisa Biedenbach, Mary Carol Kendzia.

Invitation to a Grace-Filled Journey

IF SHEER WILL had been enough to save him, my husband Scott would be alive today. Not long after surgery for an aggressive form of brain cancer, as he was moving through follow-up radiation, he was already accepting the reality that the cancer would beat him. He was realistic enough to read the literature and face the odds.

"If you die," I would begin some conversations with him, and he would gently counter, "When I die," helping me to move with him toward a peaceful death.

Which is not to say that he blindly accepted his "fate." Sometimes, in a tone of awe rather than anger, he would wonder, "Why was I chosen for this type of cancer?"

"Chosen by whom, or what?" I would counter, challenging his theology of death and dying with my firm conviction that God did not cause suffering to some end, though he persisted in clinging to the notion that there was a purpose in his illness and eventual death.

Three months after his diagnosis and soon after his death, my theology began unraveling and I found myself wondering, "Why was I chosen for this?"

Over the years since Scott's death in 1999, I have time and again recognized the wordless expression on the faces of friends at my college and in my parish, as they grappled with the same questions: "Why me?"

"Was there a reason for this?" "What could we have done to switch tracks midway in the journey so that the course of our marriage did not dead-end at this final stop that was never on the itinerary as we planned our lives together?"

After initial waverings, I have reclaimed the theology I shared with Scott during his illness: God does not choose anyone for a life of illness and suffering. Illness happens. Death sometimes follows illness. Good and unsuspecting men and women transform from wife and husband to widow and widower, often with little warning.

Just as I am sure that we are never "chosen" by God for a life of extraordinary challenges, I also firmly believe that we do have choices, once we emerge from the blessed fog that allows us to move through daily duties and relationships immediately after our loss. These choices allow us to move on and make a meaningful life, despite our sadness.

My role model for choosing to move on is Elizabeth Ann Seton, a saint with whom I have always identified, and whom I have come to admire for the many roles we share: devoted daughter, sister, friend, mother, wife, widow, religious sister, teacher—and writer.

And what a writer she was: prolific and graceful, a woman with a voice. Her story may be unfamiliar to you, so here are the essentials. Daughter of a prominent New York physician in the late eighteenth century, Elizabeth married into a well-to-do shipping family, only to watch the family business decline, mirrored by the swift physical deterioration of her beloved husband, William.

While traveling to Italy in hopes of reversing the effects of his tuberculosis, she watched his life slip away in a dank holding cell on the shores of Leghorn, Italy, where the couple and their oldest daughter were retained by Italian officials for fear that they were bringing disease into the country. A few days after the quarantine was lifted, he died, and, according to the laws of Italy, was buried the next day.

What we have in Elizabeth's writings—they have been collected into four volumes—is a poignant account of the physical and spiritual challenges she faced during that soul-wrenching period of her life. As a writer, I admire the openness and pain in the journals and letters from those days.

As a writer who is also a widow, I marvel at the direction her writing took after William's death. Only briefly, usually when she is recounting the deaths of others (her sister-in-law and "soul sister," Rebecca, as well as two daughters who preceded her in death) do we realize that she must be reliving the pain of her descent into widowhood.

As someone who knows that my husband's death was a pivotal and transforming moment in my life, I am in awe at Elizabeth's ability to move on: to raise her five children as a single mother; to work through the difficult decision to leave Trinity Episcopalian Church, the church of upper-class New Yorkers and the cradle of her deep spirituality, and to embrace Catholicism, the scorned faith of the poor and immigrants; to found a religious community, the Sisters of Charity, and to nurture the minds and souls of the young women in the school she started in a valley in Maryland, far from the energizing city of her childhood and young married life.

I have no doubt that William's death shaped her life and spirituality in ways similar to the impact Scott's death had on me. I know from her early letters how she reveled in her deep friendship and the joys of parenthood with William, whom she called in various passages "my dearest treasure," "my Dearest William," "my Dear love," and "my Seton."

Without ignoring or rejecting the pain of her loss, Elizabeth found the strength to move on.

This book, too, is about moving on. As widows and widowers, we have little choice but to do so. There are no right or wrong choices on this journey toward healing, as there is no playbook or script to guide us through the sadness, bewilderment, anger and pain—emotional and sometimes physical—we experience because of our loss.

With our choices come graces. God will not abandon us as we walk through this arid valley of death. So this book is also about graces we will encounter along the journey, if we stay open to them.

As you move through this book, and your grief, may you find consolation in the words of Elizabeth Seton: "He gives us every grace…this grace is able to carry us through every obstacle and difficulty."[1]

CHAPTER ONE

Finding "the Light From Within"

Why do you hide your face?

Why do you forget our affliction and oppression?

For we sink down to the dust;

our bodies cling to the ground.

Rise up, come to our help.

Redeem us for the sake of your steadfast love.

—Psalm 44:24–26

FAMILY AND FRIENDS tell me that the Mass of Christian Burial for Scott was the perfect liturgy to honor his nearly fifty-three years of loving and giving. I remember planning it, my daughters and several sisters gathered around our dining room table, where every Sunday Scott had inked in answers to the *New York Times* crossword puzzle. I remember choosing the songs, readings, lectors, and Eucharistic ministers.

And I still vividly remember details of his Mass: my friend, a Congregationalist minister, coaxing me to laugh by repeating an over-heard conversation about his role in the liturgy ("He's giving the homily and he's not even Catholic"); a friend of many years rescuing Scott's brother, who realized minutes before the beginning of Mass that he would not make it through his designated "Love is patient, love is kind" reading; my wheelchair-bound and slightly deaf mother commenting in a too-loud voice during the opening notes of "O Danny Boy" on the flute: "I think I'm going to cry."

I remember that I did not cry—and was told by one sister that I was the epitome of grace and graciousness. I prayed the prayers and sang any songs that I could get through without choking up. But I found little consolation in the words, the music, or the familiar patterns of the Mass. It was only in the months and years after the funeral that I came to realize the blessings of prayer and religious rituals (especially celebration of the Eucharist) as essential to my healing.

Scott died on October 26. Like many parishes, mine marks All Souls Day, November 2, with a memorial prayer service. Now, I am glad one of my sisters convinced me to attend with her, since I had been unsure whether I was up to the emotional toll it would take on me, occurring within a week of burying my husband.

It was the right decision—to be embraced by family and surrounded by a community of fellow mourners and their supporters. The altar and the steps below glowed with dozens of memorial candles, each inscribed with the name of a parishioner's relative who had died within the previous year. I was among the freshest of the grief-stricken.

Despite the occasion that forced us all to relive illness and death, I was struck by the tranquility in the worship space. This ritual ceremony was the first of many occasions in the years to come when ceremonies would gently remind me that the end of earthly life was not the end of life for Scott or for me. The candles that were lit that evening not only called to mind those who were no longer with us, but also challenged the survivors not to allow sorrow to snuff out the very faith that had sustained us to this point.

A little over a year after Scott's death, I attended another funeral Mass, my mother's. The two of them had been good friends, and had bonded even more over their illnesses. Just before Scott's diagnosis of brain cancer, my mother had been through radiation for a nonmalignant tumor at the stem of her brain to try to slow its growth. As if to seal the bond between my mother and my husband, his radiation was scheduled for the treatment center where she was just finishing up, with the same staff. Mom joked that she had "warmed up the table" for him.

My experience at my mother's funeral liturgy a year after Scott's death was a richer, more prayerful experience than Scott's had been. I had been through a year of grief, a year of weekly celebrations of Eucharist. More importantly, I was keenly aware that the Eucharist had been central to my mother's quiet spirituality. For much of her life, until illness slowed her down, she was a daily communicant, and often on Sundays would carry Communion to Catholics in a nearby nursing home. I knew the Eucharist was the perfect way to honor my mother's life in her death.

So many poignant details of her Mass of Christian Burial remain vivid: her six daughters draping the casket with the funeral pall, my niece leading the congregation in musical responses, and the whole congregation sending her off with one of her favorite hymns, "How Great Thou Art."

Rituals Are Healing

Beyond the Catholic liturgy specific to funerals, which my Catholic and non-Catholic friends consider a marvelous send-off to mark the passage from this life to life beyond death, each celebration of the Eucharist contains a richness of meaning that helped assuage my pain in the years after Scott's death. Each celebration nurtured me through its connection to community and its reliance on symbols and words.

The first Sunday after a spouse's funeral can be a turning point for the widowed: Do I return to my own church or go elsewhere? To those not in the widowed ranks, the decision may be obvious—of course, you want to worship with those who have helped you through the stages of illness and dying or who strengthened you in the face of sudden loss. That very bond is why some survivors take their time about returning: there is such a personal connection to the community that the outpouring of emotion and attention can be overwhelming.

For me there was no choice. This was the parish I had grown to love over the last dozen years, where my children had first participated in the sacrament of the Eucharist, where the wake and funeral for my husband had taken place. This was my community of worship, a community that would pray with me on my healing journey.

Although the interior of the church has been renovated recently, it was not a beautiful church at the time of Scott's death. Visitors often remarked on the starkness of the cinderblock walls, but I rarely noticed them. What comforted me were the traditions and rituals that I came to appreciate, the blending of natural elements foundational to so many religions—light and darkness, fire and water—with the human activities of washing, anointing, breaking bread, sharing a cup, embracing another in a gesture of peace.

Writing about rituals on the Hospice Foundation website, Alice Parsons Zulli explains how important ritual is in the healing process. "Ritual is sacred. Rituals can help to restore balance to life.... It is natural to express ourselves with physical actions. Death and grief are experiences that may make us feel helpless or out of control as emotional and physical energy is thrown out of balance. Rituals or ceremonies link physical and mental expression in a way that allows us to express and act out feelings and beliefs."[2]

It wasn't until years after Scott's death that I realized that it was partly the rituals embedded in every Eucharist that helped restore a sense of balance to my life. Much like the old Holiday Inn ad campaign, "The best surprise is no surprise," no matter which Mass I chose, no matter which celebrant was presiding, I knew what to expect in the order of the Mass and its symbols.

The first Advent following Scott's death, I looked forward to the simple opening hymn, sung a cappella by the congregation, four Sundays in a row, the melody and words a soothing mantra for my hurting spirit. Every Sunday I knew when to sit, kneel, and stand, during a period in which making even the smallest decisions drained me. Making the Sign of the Cross near the beginning of Mass, bowing my head in blessing, holding hands with strangers during the Our Father, extending my hand during the Sign of Peace—all were rote during the first months, but gradually I began to treasure their significance each Sunday.

Several years into widowhood, I made a commitment that I had been considering for years: I volunteered to become a regular minister of the Word at Sunday liturgies. It was such an obvious ministry for an English teacher who was in awe of the power of the Word. Already a reader during liturgies at the Catholic college where I teach, I began to look forward to the regularity of this parish commitment, once or twice a month at the 11:30 A.M. Mass.

In the orientation for new lectors, one of our deacons not only taught us how to approach the altar and articulate the text while standing at the microphone, but more importantly shared his own powerful experience of reading Scripture. "It is not just a role you assume as part of a ministry," he said. "It will transform your life."

The workbook for lectors we received became a powerful tool to help rekindle a love for Scripture that had taken a back seat to my other interests and prayer forms over the years. Each commitment to reading the welcome commentary before Mass or one of the readings on a Sunday was also a commitment to prepare all the readings for the Sunday, as well as to study the commentaries on each, in case I needed to pinch hit for a missing reader. It was also an opportunity to understand the context of the Scripture passage I would read.

The book advised lectors to prepare at least a Sunday ahead to have time during the week to pray over the reading. Although I rarely remembered this advice in time, I often pulled out the workbook the day before and would read and mull over the passages.

What I rediscovered was how breaking open the Word, sitting with it, or pondering it over a long walk brought a relevance and richness to my life that I had been missing. Before I was married, I had spent some time as a religious sister. During those years Scripture had been an intimate part of every day: We rose before dawn for morning prayer filled with the poetry of the psalms, listened prayerfully to Scripture at Mass, spent time alone reading (sometimes the Bible, sometimes books commenting on biblical texts), and closed the day with Scripture-rich vespers.

Would I have volunteered to be a lector if Scott had not died? It's a question I can't answer, of course, but it intrigues me. Maybe later, after the children were all grown and out of the house, when weekend schedules would be more predictable, or maybe when I decided to slow down and let go of some of my other busyness. Looking back on my decision, I remember it as a persistent nudge, a faint calling to move beyond my love of words to commit to proclamation of the Word.

Occasionally parishioners whom I don't know will stop me after Mass to comment on how well I read. I nod in thanks, knowing that as much as my reading has been inspiring to them in their worship experience, it has done the same for my own life. I am grateful for the whisper of a calling that led me to this ministry. Even on my "off Sundays," Scripture had been an important thread in my spiritual journey as a widow. If I should change parishes, I don't know if I will "re-up" as a lector, but I am certain that the Word of God will remain part of my continuing path toward wholeness.

Finding a Voice in Prayer

In the weeks and months after Scott's death, I discovered a new weakness in myself. Always articulate, always clever, at times I found myself at a loss for words, true words to capture my loss and my emotions. As a teacher of writing, I was fond of quoting Ernest Hemingway's advice to writers: "All you have to do is write one true sentence. Write the truest sentence that you know." Here was the stumbling block: I didn't really know what the truth about my loss was yet. I could not find the words.

C.S. Lewis did not have that problem. Known to most readers as the British author of the well-known Chronicles of Narnia (including *The Lion, the Witch and the Wardrobe*) and *The Screwtape Letters*, he found solace in words after the death of his wife, Joy. In one book, he traces his spiritual crisis through handwritten journals, which he published under a pseudonym just before his death as *A Grief Observed.*

At the beginning of his fourth journal, he writes that this will be the last because he can't go on endlessly dealing with his grief through writing. "I resolve to let this limit my jottings," he writes. "I *will not* start buying books for the purpose. In so far as this record was a defence against total collapse, a safety-valve, it has done some good." Throughout the book, he observes not only his grief for his wife, Joy, but his struggles with God. Near the beginning, he asks the question many bereaved ask:

> Meanwhile, where is God? This is one of the most disquieting symptoms. When you are happy, so happy that you have no sense of needing Him, so happy that you are tempted to feel His claims upon you as an interruption, if you remember yourself and turn to Him with gratitude and praise, you will be—or

so it feels—welcomed with open arms. But go to Him when your need is desperate, when all other help is vain, and what do you find? A door slammed in your face, and a sound of bolting and double bolting on the inside.... After that, silence.[3]

Lewis does not pray in the book, but it is clear that in his pain he is questioning and challenging God. Though I was fascinated reading such an articulate rendering of a loss of a loved one, not entirely dissimilar from mine, I needed to find a way to pray. I needed to find the right words, and I was fairly certain they would not be mine.

How could I find the words for prayer? Did I even need words to pray, since Psalm 139 assured me that the Lord has "searched me and known me," that God discerns my thoughts from far away, and that "even before a word is on my tongue," God knows it completely?

In the days after Scott's death, a spiritual mentor who had counseled me and prayed with me during Scott's brief illness advised me to turn to the psalms. I took her advice and found solace in centuries-old prayers that seemed to give words to my unspeakable sorrow.

Scripture scholar Walter Brueggemann explains the appeal of these song/prayers: "The Psalms, with a few exceptions, are not the voice of God addressing us. They are rather the voice of our own common humanity, gathered over a long period of time; a voice that continues to have amazing authenticity and contemporaneity.... We add a voice to the common elation, shared grief, and communal rage that beset all of us."

Before we can understand psalms as prayers, he writes, we need to understand the rhythms of a life of faith. Brueggemann suggests this schema in our relation to God: "being securely *oriented*, being painfully *disoriented*, and being surprisingly *reoriented*." While we all yearn to be in the first stage, that's not likely how our lives will unfold. Some of the most powerful prayer occurs when we are disoriented, when our life is in chaos—an apt description for at least the initial period in the life of a surviving spouse.

Some of the most poignant psalms to pray as a widow are the lament psalms. Brueggemann reminds us of the most famous: Psalm 22, Psalm 13, and Psalm 88. He cautions us not to

> make these psalms too "religious" or pious. Most of the lament psalms are the voices of those who "are mad as hell and are not going to take it any more." They are not religious in the sense that they are courteous or polite or deferential. They are religious only in the sense that they are willing to speak this chaos to the very face of the Holy One. Thus the lament psalm, for all its preoccupation with the hard issues at hand, invariably calls God by name and expects a response.[4]

When I pray the psalms, I do not follow a formal method for prayer. Often I read and reread them before I take a one- or two-mile walk in a nearby park. I let the images and emotions that the words evoke roll over me and articulate my sorrow. I share in the psalmist's lament in Psalm 13:

> How long, O LORD? Will you forget me forever?
>   How long will you hide your face from me?
> How long must I bear pain in my soul,
>   and have sorrow in my heart all day long?
> How long shall my enemy be exalted over me?
>
> Consider and answer me, O LORD my God!
>   Give light to my eyes, or I will sleep the sleep of death…
>   —Psalm 13:1–3

When I prayed lament songs as a young novice during morning or evening prayer, lines like the above felt overly dramatic, extreme. As a widow, they named exactly how I felt, though I would never have shared this with anyone who had not experienced a loss similar to mine: they may have judged me hysterical. As Brueggemann says, the lament psalms "express the pain, grief, dismay, and anger that life is not good" and they do this while engaging in "enormous hyperbole."

Good poetry deals in images, in metaphor. One of my favorite images that kept recurring to me during Scott's illness, an illness I gradually acknowledged to myself would not end well, comes from an Emily Dickinson poem, in which she describes her physical reaction to noticing a snake, "a narrow Fellow in the Grass" where she is walking. She writes that she

> …never met this Fellow
> Attended, or alone
> Without a tighter breathing
> and Zero at the Bone—[5]

She has named the icy fear striking at my heart during the days after Scott's diagnosis and surgery. With similar precision, the author of Psalm 6 captures the physical effect of grief:

> Be gracious to me, O LORD, for I am languishing;
>   O LORD, heal me, for my bones are shaking with terror.
> My soul also is struck with terror,
>   while you, O LORD—how long?
>
> Turn, O LORD, save my life;
>   deliver me for the sake of your steadfast love.
> For in death there is no remembrance of you;

in Sheol who can give you praise?

I am weary with my moaning;
    every night I flood my bed with tears;
    I drench my couch with my weeping.
My eyes waste away because of grief;
    they grow weak because of all my foes.

                        —Psalm 6:2–7

But the journey from grief to new life has bright moments too. At turning points, when I felt some of my physical pain of loss diminishing, when I found comfort in the embrace of a friend, when I realized I had bottomed out and was on the way up, I also turned to the psalms, the ones Brueggemann labels "psalms of celebration." At some point the chaos and disorientation begin to shift toward a surprising "reorientation." "This is not an automatic movement that can be presumed or predicted," he writes. "Nor is it a return to the old form, a return to normalcy as though nothing had happened. It is rather 'all things new.' When it happens, it is always a surprise, always a gift of graciousness, and always an experience that evokes gratitude."[6]

At these moments of surprise, graciousness, and gratitude, the psalmists supply words. In Psalm 16, we pray:

I bless the LORD who gives me counsel;
    in the night also my heart instructs me.
I keep the LORD always before me;
    because he is at my right hand, I shall not be moved.

Therefore my heart is glad, and my soul rejoices;
    my body also rests secure.
…

You show me the path of life.

In your presence there is fullness of joy;

in your right hand are pleasures forevermore.

—Psalm 16:7–9, 11

The author of Psalm 30 suggests an image that resonates with me, a metaphor that captures the transition from moving through loss with a burdensome gait to a future that promises a dance of new life:

…Weeping may linger for the night,

but joy comes with the morning.

…

You have turned my mourning into dancing;

you have taken off my sackcloth

and clothed me with joy,

so that my soul may praise you and not be silent.

O LORD my God, I will give thanks to you forever.

—Psalm 30:5, 11–12

I remember the psalms in terms similar to C.S. Lewis's gratitude for his empty journal. He used his writing as "a safety-valve," a way to unleash the pressures of sadness, uncertainty, and fears for the future. They are not the only prayers in time of grief, but they got me through some of the worst days when I was looking for the presence of God during a dark time in my life.

Negotiating the Dark Days

The dark days were there at first for me as for others who lose a spouse. I was assured by wise friends that every grief is different, though they would gladly have offered me a time-tested prescription for my return to spiritual health after the death of a spouse, to an earlier time before my world shifted from relative equilibrium to disorientation. For some, anger at their loss is transferred to God, and religion seems like a meaningless endeavor, not worth the effort. Some bereaved find consolation in liturgy, prayer, meditation, time alone.

If you play sports or exercise, you know how important it is have a strong physical core. Likewise, if you neglect your spiritual core in the aftermath of your spouse's death, you may be weaker in the long run. It's important not to deny your spiritual pain, but it's helpful to hold out hope that the intensity of it won't last forever. Regular spiritual pulse checks may help you realize that you are slowly on the mend.

One tool for checking in on your spiritual health is an assessment developed by Richard Groves, cofounder of the Sacred Art of Living Center and former director of spiritual caregiving at Hospice of Bend in Oregon. This one-page assessment focuses on four dimensions of spiritual pain: meaning, forgiveness, relatedness, and hope. For each of the four areas, Groves provides descriptors on a scale of 1 to 5. For example, under "meaning" *1* is described as "Life is filled with purpose and meaning," whereas *5* suggests "Life has become meaningless." Optional questions follow each of the four categories, for example, "What is giving me life and energy right now?" and "Who or what keeps me from being fully alive?"

Groves advises that completing the form once may not be enough. He instructs the user to "record and compare answers at regular intervals in order to discover patterns of spiritual health or distress." And, although this may be hard to believe for someone in early stages of mourning, he also counsels "trust that awareness is the first step toward healing. Instead of trying to fix spiritual pain, it only needs to be listened to and received."[7]

In the earliest days and months after a spouse's death, we may distrust the suggestion that the pain does not need to be "fixed," just "listened to and received." We just want it to go away! But relief from constant sadness, though gradual, is possible. The proof is in the pew near you during Sunday liturgy, on a park bench in quiet meditation, on walking trails and bike paths—there you will find surviving spouses who have been to the abyss yet still cling to spiritual beliefs. This, despite, or maybe because of, the spiritual pain they have moved through. They are the spiritually beautiful, the inner-lit ones captured in this reflection by Elisabeth Kübler-Ross: "People are like stained-glass windows. They sparkle and shine when the sun is out, but when darkness sets in, their true beauty is revealed only if there is light from within."[8]

Reflection Points

• Go to Richard F. Grove's website, www.sacredartofliving.org, and download the Spiritual Health Assessment. Spend some quiet time in reflection or prayers, then complete the form. Save it, and revisit the website in a month or two to mark your spiritual healing.

• Turn to the book of Psalms, using your favorite translation of the Bible. Skim through several prayers, then choose one to spend time with. Let the words of lament and hope speak to you as you connect the psalmist's universal words to your private grief.

Role Model: Elizabeth Ann Seton

Although she is now a saint, Elizabeth Ann Seton was a human who knew the pain of many losses, one of the most devastating being the death of her beloved husband, William, father to her five children. In this poignant passage recorded in her journal at his death, you may find echoes of your own spiritual pain: "Oh Oh Oh what a day.—close his eyes, lay him out, ride a journey, be obliged to see a dozen people in my room till night—and at night crowded with the whole sense of my situation—O MY FATHER, and MY GOD."[9] Yet, she weathered this and other spiritual crises in large part by relying on the comfort of the Eucharist and the consolation of personal prayer.

Prayer

Loving God, be with me in this time of sadness, pain, and uncertainty. I feel disoriented, and hunger for a time before death transformed my life. Hold me gently in the palm of your hand. Help me to believe that this pain is temporary, and that after darkness, I will find light and peace.

CHAPTER TWO

That First Year: Big Decisions

We waited while She passed—
It was a narrow time—
Too jostled were Our Souls to speak
At length the notice came.

She mentioned, and forgot—
Then lightly as a Reed
Bent to the Water, struggled scarce—
Consented and was dead—

And We—We placed the Hair—
And drew the Head erect—
And then an awful leisure was
Belief to regulate—[10]

—Emily Dickinson

EMILY DICKINSON KNEW death. Every woman living in the 1800s in the United States did, many losing mothers, sisters, and friends during childbirth on a regular basis. Although she never married, Dickinson was a watcher at enough death beds that in one of her poems she chastises God, dismissing his role as "Father!" and naming him "Burglar!" for robbing her of dear friends.

Although my college students regularly complain about Dickinson's "depressing" poems, possibly because they have not known death or want to avoid contemplating it, Dickinson can poetically articulate many of the aspects of death familiar to those of us who have lost a spouse. The days and weeks following the death may feel like "an awful leisure," especially if the illness of a spouse has dragged on for months or years, with the caregiver focusing much of daily living on just getting through each hectic, anxious day.

On the other hand, something about the pace of life picks up as survivors confront myriad practical and financial decisions. In conversations with friends whose spouses have died, three topics emerge as the most pressing and time-consuming during the first year: keeping the family together, making strategic financial decisions, and dealing with insurance companies over bills and continuing coverage.

The immediate practical family challenges vary according to family dynamics, the age of children and, sometimes, the gender of the surviving spouse. In a chapter entitled "It's a Fact—Men Are Capable of Parenthood" in *The Widower*, coauthor Willard K. Kohn writes that the transition from coparent to single parent of six daughters, ages eleven to nineteen, was cushioned by his wife Beth's extended illness. "The children and I became used to her absence; we thus became conditioned to her final absence. Also, prior to her illness, Beth had worked full-time, and so our daughters already had shared the responsibility of the home and meal preparations."

For their family, child care was not a pressing issue. "Because of their ages, no special arrangements were necessary to take care of them. We were twice blessed by the availability of Beth's sister, Mic, and my mother."

The lives of other widowers interviewed for the book did not run as smoothly as Kohn's after the death of their children's mother, according to coauthor Jane Burgess Kohn, a sociologist, now Willard's wife. Men may have to step into unfamiliar roles, such as attending PTA meetings, where one father reported feeling "as strange as hell the first few times."

Another man, Jim, describes the ordeal of finding appropriate child-care for his three young children: "When my wife died, my children were fourteen months, three, and eleven years of age. In the help field, it would have been nice if my relatives had helped. Thinking, I suppose that I would make it anyway, they never did. This was tougher than hell. My wife's brothers and sisters crossed me off shortly after the funeral. They thought I would go right out and find myself another wife to care for my children. The problem of finding babysitters and someone to watch the children was like a nightmare."[11]

When my friend Barbara was widowed suddenly at age forty-three, her first concern was the welfare of her seven children, ranging in age from four to twenty. How could she keep the family together under the same roof? One of her goals was to stay home without getting a job for a year, until the youngest began kindergarten.

At first, she had no real sense of where to begin, but she did know that she had to figure out her finances. Her social worker husband Steve had earned only a modest salary, so his life insurance, double his salary, wouldn't last long. While Barbara had worked part time in a local department store during the Christmas season for extra gift money, she had also taken care of the family finances when Steve was alive. So, she said, "I was not shocked when the gas and electric bill arrived." Still, keeping track of deadlines for all the bills became a major priority for the family's survival.

When Steve died, their family home was almost paid for after twenty-one years of marriage. At one point within the first year after Steve's death, she "seriously considered moving into an apartment or a smaller home" to help generate some cash for living expenses, but realized this was one major decision that could wait.

Other decisions regarding family patterns and dynamics began emerging as crucial. Calling a family meeting, Barbara laid out her expectations. The first was that the three oldest would return to college after the Christmas break, shortly after Steve died.

"We valued a college education for all our children, so I told them even if their grades dropped the following semester, they would get out of bed and go to every class." School was part of the fabric of their lives, and they needed the structure that classes would provide.

More subtle were the family dynamics that Barbara tried to maintain. "Trying to be Mom and Dad at the same time" was a conscious decision on her part.

"I had always been the disciplinarian, while Steve was the one who would give in and say, 'Okay, you can stay up late to watch this show, just tonight,'" Barbara remembers. She knew that she would have to alter some of her firm stances to soften the sting of her children's loss.

Stretching the family budget came easily. Even when Steve was alive, they had lived frugally to support a family of nine on his salary. She laughs about the "normal" in their household as the family grew: "With seven children, each got six ravioli out of the bag."

"We never went out to dinner when Steve was alive, that's just the way it was," says Barbara. "After he died I made sure we had enough money to order pizza once a week, just to blow some money."

Although she had to be vigilant about finances that first year, early on she made it clear to her older children that she never expected them to contribute any money they earned to keep the family solvent.

"When I told my oldest son that he would still be my son and would never have to worry about taking care of the family finances, I could tell by the relieved expression on his face that he had already been worrying and that I had removed that burden," she says.

Despite her careful planning and management, Barbara was aware that they would never have made it without Social Security survivor benefits. "I knew the checks for the children would be arriving soon, and when they did it made a huge difference," she remembers.

Help With the First Steps

My best financial advice after my husband's death came from an unexpected source: John, my brother-in-law and friend. He had already stepped in to help with end-of-life concerns when Scott was admitted to the intensive care unit and the prognosis looked grim. John urged me to leave ICU and get to the nearby branch of my bank to withdraw money from accounts, just to be sure I had enough money. He also visited local funeral homes, even pricing coffins so I would know what expenses I was facing ("The 'Barkley' is nice, but pricey," he told me with a smile), and suggested a cemetery he thought my daughters and I might feel comfortable visiting.

The real blessing soon after the funeral was John's persistence, in the face of my exhaustion and grief, that we make an appointment at a local Social Security Administration office so the children could begin drawing benefits. While Scott was alive we had been living on two salaries. Since his surgery his company had been providing disability payments; the day he died, we received his last paycheck.

Although we had never lived extravagantly, we weren't as frugal as Barbara's family. Two of my three daughters were in Catholic schools, and there were some hefty educational expenses. Like Barbara, I knew any dramatic change in their schools would affect their circle of friends, and might be detrimental to their healthy transition from having two parents to one. Social Security seemed the obvious safeguard of some degree of economic normalcy.

Within a few weeks of Scott's funeral, John and I were sitting in the lobby of the Social Security office. I had all the paperwork with me to begin the process, including the all-important death certificate.

That visit was one of many to come that would plunge me into the reality of my new state. Our family had never relied on any income except my own and Scott's. If Social Security survivor's benefits felt like a "handout" at first, I soon realized that the benefits were a tribute to the many physically and emotionally challenging years Scott had spent in the television news business as a photographer. The girls and I were always proud of his job and his somewhat public status in the local and international community because of all the well-known people he interacted with.

But we had also adjusted to a less-than-routine family life that included late night phone calls to cover homicides or fires in the city, his overnight stays at the news station during blizzards, and his occasional weeks of little contact when he was out of the country on trips shooting news features. Yes, he had earned this money, and these benefits would be his continuing financial support for his "girls," even after his death.

The Social Security counselor couldn't have been gentler. He had to deliver the requisite admonitions, such as, "This money is meant to provide housing, food, and clothing for your children, not to be spent on luxury cruises," but in him I found a compassion that I had not expected in the stereotypical "paper pusher" public employee. He assured me that the payments for the two younger girls (the oldest had just turned eighteen, so was not eligible) would be deposited electronically into my bank account on Scott's birthday, December 8.

As the bills piled up, including credit card charges to pharmacies for a series of expensive drugs that our insurance plan required us to pay for and then apply for reimbursement, I became increasingly anxious about our financial situation. December 8 could not come soon enough.

In an effort to continue the family practice of making birthdays special, I planned dinner out at a modestly priced restaurant in a nearby mall to note their late father's birthday. It would be a sad occasion without Scott, but I had purchased small Christmas ornaments for each of them, modifying his practice of choosing a special ornament for me each Christmas, always one that included three of something—carolers, bunnies, birds—a nod to our three precious daughters.

As we were waiting in the lobby, I quickly made a trip to the ATM, wondering if the promised money had been deposited. When I noted the balance in my account, I knew the money had come through, and we would be back on a more even keel for a few years. The tears that welled up were tears of grief—missing Scott on what would have been his fifty-third birthday—mingled with tears of joy and gratitude for my brother-in-law's persistence in pushing me to do what seemed painful at the time, but proved to be one more safety net to get us through the first year.

Of the important decisions the surviving spouse has to make within the first few months, the most crucial is applying for Social Security, according to financial advisor Mark Kleespies.

"We counsel our clients who have lost a spouse to slow down and process the grief, and not make any important decisions the first year," he says. Two exceptions: you should order death certificates right away, as many as ten, and apply for Social Security survivor benefits, especially if the family includes dependent children.

In the absence of a friend or relative in the know about Social Security or a financial advisor already working with your family's finances, a helpful guide through the process is the Social Security Administration page on the Internet: www.socialsecurity.gov.

The site explains that "the value of the survivors insurance you have under Social Security is probably more than the value of your current life insurance.... When you die, certain members of your family could be eligible for benefits based on your earnings."[12] These include widows, widowers (and divorced widows and widowers), children, and dependent parents.

Although the payments and eligibility will vary according to the age of the deceased, the age of the surviving spouse, and the age of the children, the website will walk you through eligibility in easy-to-read prose.

If you or your children were not receiving any Social Security benefits at the time of your spouse's death, as was the case in my family, the website includes details about how to apply (by phone or in person at a local office) as well as a helpful list of original or certified documents the survivor needs to supply:

- proof of spouse's death
- your Social Security number as well as that of your deceased spouse
- your birth certificate
- your marriage certificate
- your divorce papers (if you are applying for benefits as a divorced widow or widower)
- dependent children's Social Security numbers and birth certificates
- the deceased's W-2 forms
- the name of your bank and account number for direct deposit.

Looking back on those weeks after Scott's death, I wonder how I had the presence of mind and the energy to gather up all these documents.

Physically and emotionally drained, the last thing I wanted to do was to go through our documents at home and in a safety deposit box at the bank. Now that I realize what a godsend those Social Security bank deposits were, I am sure that my family's life, already in upheaval, could have been even worse if we had been forced to make major changes because of a lack of money.

Money Matters

As much as I valued my brother-in-law's practical nudging, I knew he could not help with other important, though not as urgent, financial decisions. Fortunately, during Scott's illness and after his death, we had been blessed with assistance from our parish's Helping Hands Ministry, volunteers who "share their time and talent to offer meals, transportation, and other temporary, practical assistance during times of illness and other family 'challenges.'" Volunteers donated food for the reception after Scott's funeral, and provided other kindnesses. At the time, one of the cochairs happened to be Mark Kleespies, who offered initial advice about sorting through life insurance, pensions, and tax-deferred accounts (an IRA and 401(k)), and about making some secure investments at a time when the stock market was taking a dive.

Thirteen years ago, if anyone would have asked me if I needed an investment advisor, I would have replied that only wealthy people could afford them. I realize now that I cannot afford not to have one; I made the decision to stay with Mark's investment firm.

Investments are often the least concern of surviving spouses, but these persistent financial issues affect every widow or widower. In the year after her husband's death, besides stretching insurance and Social Security income for food and monthly bills, Barbara had to deal with unexpected major household purchases ("In the first four months, a water heater and a new furnace: I wondered 'How can this be happening?'"). She came to a conclusion that she gladly shares with every surviving spouse: "Find someone you can trust to help you, and not a friend or family member."

Family members, she says without discounting their good intentions, are too quick to assure you not to worry, that everything will be all right, or to respond to a request for financial advice with "Oh, I don't know, what do you think?"

"Talk to someone who doesn't love you," she goes on. "They will give you an unbiased opinion, even if it is hard to hear."

Although Barbara decided not to get financial advice from relatives, she was never afraid to ask for help. One immediate concern after her husband's death was health insurance for herself and her seven children. Fortunately, her brother owned his own company at the time of her husband's death. He put her on the payroll as a consultant so she was able to pay for medical insurance during the first year of widowhood before she accepted a job that provided that important benefit.

In my case, our family had been covered by health insurance at Scott's place of employment. Once I began working full-time nine years before his death, we decided to keep the family on his plan because the benefits were better and because we wanted to stay with the same family practitioner we had grown to trust and love. He had guided us through several of our children's illnesses, including asthma and Type 1 diabetes.

As Scott was dying I realized that one important transition I would need to make immediately was to contact the human resources office at the college where I worked to begin coverage. The day after Scott's death, I received a visit from one of his newsroom friends who delivered a message that seemed a direct gift from God: the company would continue our medical coverage for a year. No need to make the transition, no need to switch doctors.

One insurance headache avoided. I thought the path was clear.

Little did I know of the land mines that would pop up through the first year, all related to Scott's medical bills. A friend of mine whose wife had been seriously ill for several years before her death told me that when bills came in from hospitals and surgeons, he was not distracted from the important job of helping his four sons adjust to the loss of their mother because he turned the bills over to the professionals at his place of work, the human resources folks.

That never occurred to me, and it would not have worked for several reasons: I did not know the HR people at Scott's former job, although I did ask them for help a few times. More important, within a few months of Scott's death, his company changed health insurance plans. I would have to handle medical disputes on my own.

A few months ago as I was shredding old tax forms and other papers, I came across a pile of bills and paperwork for Scott. My memories flooded back, not only of his illness and death, but more to the point, of the pain of fighting with hospitals and insurers during a period when I was desperately treading water to keep my family from drowning.

The biggest challenge came soon after Scott's death. I had submitted a bill for an MRI ordered by the neurosurgeon who would perform Scott's brain surgery. Insurance rejected the claim. Their reasoning: Scott had already had one MRI, which had located the tumor, and insurance had paid for it. On the day of the second MRI, which the neurosurgeon had asked for to guide him through the complex surgery, Scott was not yet his patient. The neurosurgeon had asked us to get another MRI and bring it to his office for a consultation. Only after that visit, according to the insurance company, could the doctor have authorized the MRI.

I can only describe my continued calls and written correspondence over several months as an emotional and spiritual trial. Without exaggerating the toll it took, I can say that my unspoken prayer was "Lord, let this cup pass…and soon." Despite my passionate and articulate letters stating my case, I felt I was losing the battle over a fifteen-hundred-dollar bill, which I could not afford to pay.

I realized I could not do this alone, so I called in the big guns: My family physician, who had been more than just a doctor during the months after Scott's surgery. Several times during those months, he would call on a Sunday night, after returning from services at his church, to check on us and to assure me of his prayers. Although it took some swallowing of pride, I asked if he would step in and deal with the bill. To us he was a gentle man, but, according to overheard conversations in a hospital lobby, he was a force no one wanted to reckon with when dealing with his patients. I do not know what he wrote, but after his intervention, I never heard about that bill again.

But I heard from other health care providers whose bills were equally confusing and unfair. Most seemed the product of a complicated hospital billing system that sent me from one department to another, kept me on hold, or cut me off during conversations, probably accidentally, forcing me to listen to the automated message, "If you are trying to make a call, please hang up and try again."

When one particularly nagging bill was resolved, I took several of my friends to lunch at a favorite pizza parlor to celebrate. Unfortunately, the celebration was premature. That same charge appeared on another hospital printout soon after, and the emotionally draining phone call cycle started all over. My persistence paid off, and the three of us were back at the pizza parlor celebrating the second "resolution" of the same disputed charge.

Within a few months, every bill seemed to be cleared up. Is it any wonder, though, that I kept those bills for as long as I did, over ten years? Those several protracted insurance fights produced in me a sort of paranoia that still lingers about "unfinished financial issues" that I'm afraid will come back to haunt me even when they seem resolved.

Eventually, immediate financial and practical concerns do get resolved, as you move into the rhythm of a new state of life and possibly new family dynamics. For most surviving spouses, the end of the first year, often something to dread before it arrives, is also an occasion to celebrate in a quiet way, because you've proved you have made it to that symbolic milestone.

One of my favorite quotes from Dag Hammarskjold spoke to me in my early grief, and still speaks to me today: "The present moment is significant, not as the bridge between past and future, but by reason of its contents, contents which can fill our emptiness and become ours, if we are capable of receiving them."[13]

When we were first married, Scott's parents shared their motto in life, which we embraced as our own: "One day at a time." Those words got me through the horrific few months after Scott's surgery and before his death, and they also guided me as I navigated the challenges of that first year.

Reflection Points

• One way to stay focused on the present is to use the technique of mindful breathing. Find a quiet spot. Try to clear your mind of worries about bills, insurance, or broken appliances. For two or three minutes, breathe in deeply, then breathe out, consciously rejecting any thoughts that begin to intrude on your attention to the present moment.

• Reaching out in gratitude to those who have helped is a way of temporarily stepping outside the web of practical issues that can become all-consuming. Take a few minutes to identify one person who has helped you through the maze of tasks and decisions. Say a prayer of gratitude, or, if you feel up to it, send that person an e-mail or card with a brief message of thanks.

Role Model: Barbara Lange Kallmeyer

Left with seven children after her husband's death, Barbara didn't have the luxury of delaying hard decisions while she worked through her grief. She had bills to pay, to put food on the table, children to care for, and more than her fair share of major and minor repairs that kept cropping up. She took advantage of counseling through Cancer Family Care ("I just dumped to get it all out. They couldn't get rid of me.") and then got on with the work ahead. "There are some hard things you have to do," she says. "You just have to gut it out."

Prayer

Loving God, be with me during these days that challenge me with new problems and challenges I would rather avoid but know I cannot. Give me the humility to ask for help when I cannot go it alone. Shower your blessings on those who are there when I most need them.

CHAPTER THREE

Letting Go, and Getting on With the Details of Life

"Somewhere deep down we know that in the final analysis we *do* decide things and that even our decisions to let someone else decide are really *our* decisions, however pusillanimous."[14]

—Harvey Cox

WITHIN WEEKS OF Scott's death, many of my evenings were spent on the floor of our walk-in closet, sorting through papers, awards, and photographs he had accumulated through his thirty-plus years as a television news photographer. Each year, at least since we had been married, he had kept an appointment calendar in which he logged sites and hours on the job, noting overtime for compensation.

His entries as early as the fall of 1998 gave a glimpse of the beginnings of his health problems, especially recurring cryptic notes about severe headaches. He had never shared his health worries, probably to protect me, so the calendar entries came as a sad revelation. I began pitching the calendars, filling our trash can weekly with his books full of jottings that had little value to me without him to interpret them.

As I shared my cleaning progress with a friend, he cautioned, "Don't get too energetic or you may regret throwing things out too soon."

Partway through the process, I saw the wisdom of his advice, but it was too late. I had located two of the three calendars for the years of my daughters' births, which Scott had proudly recorded. What had happened to the third? In my haste to move on, I'm sure I had purged too quickly and overlooked the year embossed on that missing book.

Letting go and moving on: It's a fine line for surviving spouses. At some point, after the initial difficult financial and practical details associated with death have been settled, there are still important decisions to confront, ones that concern not only the surviving spouse but also the children.

One symbolic decision that widowed friends and I weigh in on occasionally is how long we wore our wedding rings. Soon after Scott's death, a jeweler helped me creatively display my engagement ring, transforming it into a heart-shaped pendant to wear around my neck.

What to do with my wedding ring was not so clear. I was still wearing it about six months into widowhood when a male psychologist whom my daughter was seeing for depression directed a question at me: "So how long are you going to wear your wedding ring?" The curt question seemed inappropriate, given that my daughter, not I, was his client. And I resented the implication in his follow-up remarks that she would never move through grief until her mother had. A few appointments later, based on that and several other incidents, we terminated his services; I continued to wear the ring. I would know the right time when, or if, I should decide to take it off.

What else to let go of, and when? Closets full of clothing—what to do with them? One friend loaded up his SUV several times to donate his wife's clothing to an annual sale benefiting a religious order. Afterward he told me it that was the right decision, but an emotional one. Most of Scott's work clothes and shoes went to a local St. Vincent de Paul store, but I had another use for his many protective winter coats.

Over the years, he had covered news in the poorer parts of our city. One sweltering summer I remember his calling me to say that after interviewing an elderly widow in a small apartment in the inner city about living through a heat wave, he had gone to a store, bought her a fan, and delivered it to her. He was always aware of how extremes of heat and cold took their toll on the less fortunate. So in the midst of winter I gathered up his coats and took them to a local homeless shelter, knowing that his good intentions would live on, warming the bodies of those on the margins of our society.

After my mother died, my father parceled out some of the more valuable family possessions in anticipation of his move from our family home: the Christmas crèche, my grandmother's oil lamp, the family piano. The big things were easy for him, but I was surprised that he was almost paralyzed about parting with things that seemed insignificant: doilies, unmatched candles, paper cocktail napkins. My father, who over many decades had made major decisions about his family and his profession, could not decide to pitch a plastic Christmas cookie platter which still had the dollar price tag on it, and insisted I take it home—and use it.

Taking on Unfamiliar Tasks

Making decisions, trivial or major, can be burdensome for some surviving spouses. In a chapter titled "How Young Widows Have Coped with Their Problems" in *Perspectives on Bereavement*, sociologist Tamara Ferguson writes that about ten percent of the young widows she interviewed for her study

> considered that making decisions alone had been the most serious problem. The widow's need to be certain that she was making the right decision was based not only on her emotional

involvement with her husband's death but also on the fact that the structure of her family life had changed. She had been accustomed to making plans which took into account her husband's welfare, but now she had become a single woman with children who had to plan only for herself and them—it was a state of affairs which she had never experienced and it was difficult for her to know what she should do.[15]

Most of the decisions both widows and widowers make, no matter their age, are practical and, frequently, financial. Fortunately, findings reported through *The Changing Lives of Older Couples Study* are not as grim as one might think. Although "widowhood heightens one's economic vulnerability," it "rarely causes complete financial devastation for older adults," reports Rebecca L. Utz in the book *Spousal Bereavement in Late Life.*

"The negative economic consequences of widowhood were more severe for women than for men," she goes on. "About three quarters (72%) of women expected their income to decline after spousal loss, but less than a third (29%) of men held this expectation. Likewise, 7% of widows, compared to 2% of widowers, reported serious financial problems after widowhood."[16]

The women interviewed for *The Changing Lives of Older Couples Study* were sixty-five or older and had generally lived the traditional marriage model of a working husband and a stay-at-home wife. In contrast, almost all of my widowed friends, male and female, had been in marriages where each spouse contributed income to the family. Although they lost some income after the spouse's death, they were able to combine life insurance and Social Security benefits to keep family income out of the dangerous range. The bigger adjustments in their lives were the consequences of losing a partner who once shared everyday household tasks.

It comes as no surprise that the older widows and widowers in Utz's study led her to conclude that the "need to readjust household chores can be quite stressful for the bereaved. Roughly half of the bereaved men (54%) and half of the bereaved women (51%) reported feeling overwhelmed by the need to perform basic tasks such as meal preparation" and "that those persons who reported the greatest change in task performance exhibited highest levels of anxiety, depressive symptoms, and grief."[17]

But some older widows and widowers whose marriages followed traditional gender roles adapt well. Take the case of my father, Wally. He had been caring for my ailing mother at home for several years before her death. Eventually, she was too unstable on her feet to continue what she loved doing so well, cooking meals. So he took over that chore and household cleaning tasks.

After her death, he found a "mom and pop" café nearby, where he regularly ate well-balanced meals and interacted with a familiar staff. One of my sisters remembers, however, that "his cooking skills were pretty limited. I will never forget stopping in after Mom's death. He was making himself spaghetti. He had a quarter pound in a very small pot. He thought it would be done when the water was all boiled off."

When Dan's wife of forty-one years died, he was forced to shoulder alone the additional burden of the household chores they had always shared. "Not atypically, I mostly did the work outside of the home and took care of the cars," he says. "She had the heavy lifting of doing the laundry, hosting holiday meals, and paying the bills."

He describes two of the most difficult adjustments after her death: "paying the bills and doing the laundry. I really knew little about our finances, and now with doing my own books, I know, and have to do, far more work than I ever dreamed existed." The family budget had always been Donna's area; she took care of all the money, giving him "a sort of allowance. When we went to see our tax-preparer each year, she had many more comments and questions than I did and had all the paperwork he needed."

A few years before Donna's death, Dan began taking care of his mother's finances when she entered a retirement home. Even with those years under his belt, when Donna died he was unprepared for how complicated money matters actually could get.

"It's not that I'm not good at math, but it's just that as an artist I am visual, and not everything can be explained through a pie chart or bar graph," he explains. He is grateful to employees of his bank, who would explain with great patience anything he asked about money matters. One of his best friends, a biologist not a financier, "who knows everything about everything," was always generous in helping Dan figure out "what to do with money at any given time."

For Dan doing laundry was another eye-opening experience. Donna had her own very particular system for laundry, having grown up in a family that regularly ironed handkerchiefs and underwear. Helping her out would have "messed up her system of sorting colors and hanging jeans outside or inside to dry," he says. Before her death he had bought her an electronic washer and dryer, which after her death he found complicated to operate.

"In the beginning I tried to mimic Donna's method, but finally gave up and decided to just throw everything into one load," he says with a laugh. "If I put something in the dryer and it shrinks, that's okay. I've been eating less and losing weight since her death, so it doesn't matter if my clothes start getting smaller."

Thinking about my own situation, I realize what unwitting preparation for widowhood I received because my husband put in so much time at work. Throughout our marriage he took pride in caring for the yard, ironing his own clothes (I didn't quite get the creases in his pants right), and cooking for dinner guests. Some more traditional "male" roles fell to me: getting oil changes and attending to repairs of the family car (he took care of his car for work) and shoveling snow (as a teacher I got occasional "snow days" while he was putting in extra hours shooting video of people like me shoveling out from blizzards).

The big task of buying cars was one we had shared over the years. Once our children were born, we bought only one new car, a decision influenced by our financial situation and Scott's belief that new cars lost value too quickly to be a good investment. Over the years, we regularly sought car advice from Bob, a wholesale used car dealer recommended by a friend. When we were ready for a "new" car, we would specify the brand, preferred mileage, and price range—and within weeks we'd be screwing our old license plates onto our newest family car.

After Scott's death, I turned to Bob several times for car advice, following the now-familiar routine. Only once did we get a dud—and that was my fault, not his. Within a year or so after Scott's death, my daughter Katie needed a car so she could drive to the school where she was doing a teaching practicum. When I learned that it had broken down several times during trips to school, I regretted that I had asked Bob to find us something for about three thousand dollars, which was what I could scrape together without taking out another loan. I realize now that the car had been a source of anxiety to Katie when she was still grieving her father. When her little red car was rear-ended and totaled, she couldn't have been more relieved.

Cars—their upkeep and purchase—can be a source of stress for many widows. One colleague, whose husband died suddenly, was particularly vexed to find out how much her late husband still owed on his car and trucks. In the midst of the other financial and emotional issues she was facing that first year of widowhood, she had to negotiate payments and eventually the sale of those vehicles that were sitting unused. The paperwork and financial details of these transactions were a particular burden for someone who had never written a check in her life.

For another friend, though, her late husband's car was a welcome solution to children coming of driving age. "It was a piece of junk," she laughs. "But every time we got a new driver in the family, they drove Dad's old car until they could save enough money from their jobs to buy their own."

Since I have bought several cars, new and used, since Scott's death, I am getting less intimidated by some of the hard sells a woman shopping alone can encounter, if she chooses the wrong dealer. Some female friends—widowed, single, and divorced—are wise and humble enough to ask male friends to accompany them on car-seeking expeditions. Whether or not the deal is any better than it would have been if they had shopped alone is not the real issue; they just feel more comfortable with a man beside them as reinforcement as they negotiate price and financing.

If you don't have male friends you feel close enough to ask to spend several evenings or weekend afternoons car-shopping, the Internet offers some valuable resources. One is a twenty-eight page downloadable booklet called *Your Road to Confidence: A Widow's Guide to Buying, Selling and Maintaining a Car* published by The Hartford. Through focus groups with forty-five widows, researchers concluded that some of the biggest stressors in a widow's life revolve around purchasing, repairing, insuring, and driving her car.

The introduction to the pamphlet acknowledges that "there are many widows who have no need of this information. These women may have always cared for their own cars, and continue to be perfectly competent and comfortable dealing with car-related issues. More power to them—but this booklet is not meant for them."[18]

Sampling the table of contents gives a taste of the down-to-earth advice inside the booklet. Among topics covered are "Your Husband's Car—Emotional Choices," "Ten Tips on Getting the Best Deal," and "Some Important Tips for Women Driving Alone."

Sprinkled throughout this practical guide are quotes from focus group participants, giving an inkling of the range of experiences represented in the study's sample. One participant lamented: "After the breakdown I sat and cried for 20 minutes. The car just didn't go. Then I said, 'Who will I call?'"[19]

Another woman expressed admirable confidence in "playing ball" with dealers: "When they started with these scams, I'd go 'Ciao, Babe!' And I said 'If this were the last car in the world, I would not buy it from you! What don't you understand? This is what I'm going to spend, this is what I want. Either you play ball or you don't!'"[20]

What About the House?

If car purchases and repairs can strain patience and finances, homes are an even bigger source of worrisome decisions. Sometimes problems arise because the deceased has always taken care of home upkeep and repair. Sometimes the strain is more emotional: the home symbolizes years of harmony or discord with a deceased partner, a structure filled with family history and memories. At other times, the home represents financial challenges that threaten to wipe out what little income is available for the family to live on.

For Elaine, whose husband Ben had been ill with pancreatic cancer for about seventeen months before he died, the decision to move out of the house where their daughter had been born and raised was more practical than emotional.

About two years after Ben's death, having taken over his role of keeping up the property, she decided it was time to sell. "Things were going wrong with the house all the time," she says. "I was tired of cutting the grass and taking care of the lawn. And I just thought I was ready to downsize."

It was a little under two years after Donna's death when Dan began thinking about selling their family home. "The year after she died, I really didn't like being at home," he says. "She had died there, and I had witnessed her last breath in our living room."

Following the advice he has always given to his widower friends, Dan did not make any decisions about the house the first year. But now that he is in a serious dating relationship, "with a new life ahead, it is time for me to begin living in fresh surroundings which have no baggage of the past."

Sometimes the "one-year rule" is economically unfeasible to follow. Less than a year ago, a friend's husband died suddenly, leaving little insurance. The family's house payments were paid from disability checks he had been receiving, which abruptly stopped when he died. The financial advice she received and her own realism about the limited income from her job convinced her to sell the home rather than allow it to go into foreclosure.

No matter what the circumstances of leaving a home, it is often another grief experience.

Even though Elaine came to see her house without Ben as "just a place," she was surprised at her emotional reaction during the closing. The couple that bought the house reminded Elaine of what she and Ben had been like when they had moved into it years ago—young and about to start a family. "I hadn't cried much since Ben's death, but I started to cry and told them, 'I hope you're as happy in this house as we were,'" she said.

Sometimes leaving a home, neighborhood, and friends is a decision the widow or widower has no control over, as was the case with Linda's mother. While both Linda's parents were alive, they sold the family home, then built an addition on the home of one of their daughters, on the same street where they had lived and formed deep friendships over many years.

After Linda's father died, her mother transformed from the independent and convivial mother they had known to a needy woman who was "tremendously lonely," telling her children, "Nothing is fun anymore."

When the host daughter and husband decided to sell the house with the "parent addition" to move closer to children out of town, their mother was devastated. "Betrayed" is the word she used when chiding her children for pulling her from the city where so many of her friends still lived and asking her to move to another state to live with a different daughter and her family.

"Understandably, our strong-willed mother fought the move up until the actual moving day," says Linda. "Once she was in the car, though, she was okay with it, and she adapted pretty quickly to her new home."

In considering a change of location, surviving spouses need to balance the overall financial health of the family with the needs of their children, especially younger ones, who will change schools and lose friends with the move. But even grown children may experience the loss of the house as yet another reminder of the death of a parent.

When my father was ready to sell the home where he had lived for fifty years, the only home my two youngest sisters had ever known, we knew it was the right decision. He had few friends left in town, and he would be moving to the city were four of his six daughters lived.

To his credit, my father helped us through it by agreeing to host a "farewell to the homestead" cookout, where all six daughters and several of their spouses shared a simple meal, memories, toasts, and occasions for family photos, not only to say good-bye to their home but also to recall the many ways this amazing mother and wife had made this house a home. Weeks later, just before the moving van was to arrive, several of us gathered at the nearly empty house, going from room to room sharing memories and participating in a brief prayer led by our oldest sister.

One housing option that neither my father nor Linda's mother had considered but may appeal to some widows and widowers is "co-housing," an option begun in Denmark and available in the United States for several decades. According to the one organization's website,

> Cohousing is a type of collaborative housing in which residents actively participate in the design and operation of their own neighborhoods.
>
> Co-housing residents are consciously committed to living as a community. The physical design encourages both social contact and individual space. Private homes contain all the features of conventional homes, but residents also have access to extensive common facilities such as open space, courtyards, a playground and a common house.[21]

One community that makes the option look particularly attractive to older widows is the Older Women's Co-Housing group, the first co-housing community for older women in the United Kingdom. The photo on their website's "who are we" page is charming: twenty-three mostly gray-haired women, huddled together for a group photo, the smiles on their faces a witness to their achievement of one of their stated goals: "care and support for one another."

They are a self-described "group of women aged from 50 to 80+…. Their decision to be for women only is based on the fact that it tends to be women who live alone most in old age…. They want to live close to each other—with their own front doors—and offer each other mutual support as they get older. The group also wants to live in energy efficient ways and to be a resource for its local community."[22]

No matter when you face the decision to let go of your home, it is wise to consult not only a real-estate professional but also a tax advisor to negotiate the complexities of a sale. For example, in response to one widow's query posted on www.realtor.com about selling her home, a Realtor advised her that she "may qualify for short sale based on your ability to prove a 'hardship,' i.e., where you are unable to continue making payments on the mortgage." Another option would be "a loan modification which is essentially the refinancing [of] your mortgage" if the woman was interested in keeping her home. Should you decide to sell, be sure to seek counsel about tax-free profits on the sale.

According to Mary Beth Franklin, writing on kiplinger.com in 2009,

> a recent change in the law provides a special rule for widows and widowers.
>
> Previously, a surviving spouse could claim the full $500,000 exclusion [$250,000 for each spouse of tax-free profit from selling their home] only if the home was sold in the year that a joint return was filed, which generally is limited to the year the spouse dies. But now a surviving spouse may exclude up to $500,000 of profit from the sale of the principal residence if it occurs within two years of the spouse's death.[23]

In the quote that opens this chapter, theologian Harvey Cox writes about the importance of making decisions, an insight that is sometimes misquoted in abbreviated form as "Not to decide is to decide." Moving through grief to new life will of necessity include decisions at every turn: little ones—to wear or not to wear my wedding ring—to major ones that trickle down to affect children—to sell or not to sell our home. Even if we at times may lack confidence or conviction, there are decisions we can't avoid.

As Dan's story reminds us, sometimes we have to lower our standards and throw the colored and white laundry into the same load; if it discolors or shrinks, we need to be easy on ourselves, and, with a sense of humor and forgiveness, just move on. No one who is truly your friend expects all your decisions to be the "right" ones. You may be delighted to discover, as I have over and over again on my widow journey, that there are all kinds of good people out there who will come to your rescue, reminding you, "I've got your back."

Reflection Points

• You can't avoid decisions, major and minor, as you adjust to your new life without your spouse. But anxiety about those decisions can be crippling. Spend some time praying about Jesus's words in Matthew 6:27–30: "And can any of you by worrying add a single hour to your span of life? And why do you worry about clothing? Consider the lilies of the field, how they grow; they neither toil nor spin, yet I tell you, even Solomon in all his glory was not clothed like one of these. But if God so clothes the grass of the field, which is alive today and tomorrow is thrown into the oven, will he not much more clothe you—you of little faith?"

• Set aside some time this week to sort through your spouse's clothing and other possessions. What can you give away to those less fortunate than your family? Who can help you with this chore? What is important to keep—for yourself, for your children, for his or her family—as a tangible reminder of this loved one's mark on all your lives?

Role Model: Jane de Chantal

We know Jane de Chantal mainly as a founder of a religious congregation under the spiritual direction of Francis de Sales, whom she met as a young widowed mother of four children. But many ordinary experiences prepared her for her good work in religious life.

When she married Baron Christophe de Chantal, a widower, she accepted the responsibility of restoring his deteriorating castle and bringing order to their servants and finances. After his sudden death in a hunting accident, she had to deal not only with her grief but also with her anger at the friend who had accidentally shot Christophe—all the while caring for her children, the youngest barely two weeks old.

Although she longed to return to her widowed father's home, she gave in to a request from her father-in-law to help with his household in another town, where he lived with a housekeeper and several illegitimate children. The request was more a threat: come or he would cut her children out of his will. Her years there were unpleasant, but once again she brought order out of chaos, and even ran a school for her own and the other children in the chapel wing of the castle.

Prayer

Loving God, in my worries about the hard choices I'm facing, I'm in danger of forgetting your promise that you will be with me until the end of my days. I need gentle reminders about the birds of the air, whom you feed, and the lilies of the field, which you clothe in such glorious colors. Surely your grace and the support of my family and friends will help me through these bumpy times on my journey toward healing.

CHAPTER FOUR

Who's Caring for the Caregiver?

My dear Georgie,

Why haven't I written? Because, dear Georgie, I am like the dry, dead leafless tree, and have only cold, dead, slumbering buds of hope on the end of stiff, hard, frozen twigs of thought, but no leaves, no blossoms; nothing…. I am cold, weary, dead; everything is a burden to me….

I let my plants die by inches before my eyes, and do not water them, and I dread everything I do, and wish it was not to be done…. The fact is, pussy, mamma is tired. Life to you is gay and joyous, but to mamma it has been a battle in which the spirit is willing but the flesh is weak; and she would be glad… to lie down with her arms around the wayside cross, and sleep away into a brighter scene.[24]

—Harriet Beecher Stowe to her daughter, two years after the death of Stowe's second of two sons

A FEW WEEKS after Scott's death, two friends in separate encounters made comments that reminded me that it was time to start attending to my own health. The first was a male friend, a former counselor, who looked me up and down and delivered this verdict: "You're losing weight, aren't you? Too much. You need to start taking care of yourself."

The second was an older friend, who weeks into Scott's illness had taken me out for a difficult talk over dinner to let me know that chances of his recovery were slim. A scientist by training, she had researched his brain cancer, glioblastoma multiforme, and had the courage to describe for me in detail how it attacks the brain. She was all straight talk— more so than the surgeon and oncologist who were being vague enough to instill hope in me. Now, after his death, she once again invited me to dinner to explain in lay terms the workings of the human immune system, offering advice about keeping it strong: eat, sleep, and exercise.

Not long after that heart-to-heart dinner, I got an object lesson from a colleague who was serving on a search committee with me. She was also a recent widow, her husband having died suddenly from a heart attack a few weeks before Scott's diagnosis. Sitting next to her, I noticed her persistent cough, a symptom that eventually led to a diagnosis of a cancer of her immune system.

I was ready to get serious about my health, but since the onset of Scott's illness, my appetite had diminished. During the week when he was in intensive care, I took a few trips to the hospital cafeteria, but only picked at the food on my plate. To get me to eat and to lighten my spirits, my oldest sister joked, "When I get to heaven one of the first challenges I'll have for God is this business about eating and stress: thin people stop eating, and fat people just eat more and more."

Whether your spouse's illness extended over months or years or whether the death was unanticipated and sudden, your body and emotions probably have been stretched beyond their limits. You need to take positive steps to get them back to health. As you care for others around you, especially your children, it's important to remember that if you get sick, you're adding one more source of sadness to their lives.

Studies about the health of widows and widowers are generally not uplifting, but they offer you motivation to take care of yourself. "A Guide for the Newly Widowed" published on the American Association of Retired Persons (AARP) website offers this reminder: "Stress can wreak havoc on your health. The effect of grief on our health is just beginning to be measured. While guarding your health can be among the least of your concerns during the throes of grief, you must work toward maintaining your health as soon as you feel able. This means beginning some form of regular exercise, getting proper nutrition, and reporting physical complaints to your doctor."[25]

One effect of grief that has been of interest to researchers is whether grief has any measureable effect on the life expectancy of widows and widowers. In a study published in 2012 in *BMC Public Health,* a team of researchers led by Bragi Skulason assessed the survival rates of 357 widowers in Iceland. Noting that a recent study in the United States "indicated an 18% increased risk of death for widowers compared to non-widowers over a period of 9 years," they set out to discover whether widowers in their group had a greater risk of death than the general population.

Their conclusion is not heartening: "Becoming a widower is related to an increased risk of death for at least 6 to 9 years after the death of the spouse."[26] Although the authors did not pinpoint reasons, other studies showed high rates of cancer and cardiovascular disease among widowers that were most likely linked to smoking, excessive alcohol use, poor dietary habits, not enough physical activity, and obesity.

Although the outlook for widows is not as grim, a comprehensive study published in 2012 by Eran Shor and colleagues in the journal *Demography* analyzes data taken from 123 investigations about health conducted over twenty-seven years, representing five hundred million men and women in twenty-two counties. This analysis concludes that "overall, the relative risk of death for those who lost their spouse was 22% higher than the risk among married persons" [27] and that this risk has been slowly increasing over time.

As disturbing as these statistics might be to you, the good news is that there are people in your life, as there were in mine the first few years, who are eager to help you get your physical and emotional selves back on solid ground.

After dealing with an ill or dying spouse, the last person you might want to talk to is a doctor. But how long has it been since the focus of a visit to one or many doctors has been you, and not your spouse?

Dr. John Spaccarelli, who has been in family medicine for thirty-seven years and currently treats a large elderly population, recommends that within a few months of your spouse's death you schedule a visit with your doctor for a wellness exam.

During his examination of surviving spouses, he pokes around for the answer to this question: "What have they ignored about their own health during the time they've been caring for their spouse's?"

Spaccarelli is often aware of the stress the caretaker has been under, especially if the illness has been a protracted one. "Anxiety and stress lead to comments like, 'I can't sleep,' 'I can't eat,' 'I fly off the handle too often because of the demands of the situations,' 'I'm not getting enough help,'" he observes. "It's not that they're ungrateful for those who are helping them, it's just that they're worn out."

Elusive Sleep

What the bereaved, especially women, need is a good night's sleep, and many are not getting it, according to a chapter in *Spousal Bereavement in Late Life* titled "A Closer Look at Health and Widowhood: Do Health Behaviors Change After Loss of a Spouse?"

Researchers Amy Mehraban Pienta and Melissa M. Franks compared married and widowed women's sleep patterns. At the study's six-month mark bereaved persons reported "less daily sleep than their married peers. Married women get 7.8 hours of sleep per day whereas widows sleep only 7.1 hours."[28] By eighteen months there appears to be little difference in sleep patterns of the two groups. But at the six-month interview, more widows reported using sleep medication than their married peers.

When Spaccarelli writes prescriptions for sleep problems, he tells patients "not to use the medicine every night. A good night's sleep is important, but if they take it every night they might come to believe they will only be able to sleep with drugs. If they take it daily, eventually they will have to increase the dosage to notice any effect." He is also cautious about side effects and drug interactions and works to prescribe a drug that doesn't leave his patients feeling so "hungover" the next day that they can't function.

In his work with elderly patients, Spaccarelli is aware that a common factor in falls that lead to broken bones is the use of sedating drugs. So he cautions patients to make sure their evening and bedtime environment is safe. "Check to see that the route to the bathroom is clear," he advises. "Pick up throw rugs, hide loose lamp cords, and leave a light on in the bathroom at night so when you get up and are drowsy, you don't hurt yourself."

Poor nutrition is another area of concern to medical professionals who treat the widowed. "Once a spouse dies, the social aspect of a meal is gone," says Spaccarelli. "Typically widows and widowers are not eating enough. If they're eating out, often their diet is high in fat and high in salt," both potential health risks. This problem more likely affects older men if the marriage was a traditional one where the wife did most of the cooking.

Another trouble spot related to nutrition, especially for men, is the use of alcohol. Under the leadership of János Pilling, a research team studied 466 bereaved men and women in Hungary, 14.3% of them widows and widowers, to examine connections between grief and alcohol. The three-year study considered several factors: the amount and frequency of alcohol use, as well as dependence and side effects. The team concluded that alcohol use among bereaved men is a problem during the initial years of bereavement.

"Although alcohol is a maladaptive way of coping, in spite of its risks it is one of the traditional forms of reducing stress in western society," the study points out. "Women express their feelings more overtly than men, therefore men are more at risk to resort to drink in order to relieve stress."[29]

A few years ago a phone conversation with a male friend brought home to me the dangers of using alcohol as a coping mechanism. Having renewed a pair of season tickets to a theater before his wife's death, he asked me if I would go to the first play with him. That was fine: I liked him, and I enjoy live theater. What I thought was going to be one play turned into the whole season. It must have been clear to him that I was trying to keep the relationship platonic; it was also clear to me that my friend was lonely.

One night he called late to talk about a college class he was planning to teach, but his comments were sprinkled with sexual innuendoes that I found surprising and a bit unnerving. In an e-mail the next morning, I told him how offended I was. His response did not surprise me: He was sorry. He had been working on the course and had begun drinking too early and too much. "Once you start," he had told me in an earlier conversation, "what reason is there to stop?"

I understood. During our marriage, Scott and I had prefaced many meals with a "kid-free happy hour" to catch up on each other's days. During his illness we curtailed drinking because of his medications. A few years after his death, once my children were fairly independent, I began drinking more than I admitted. The long nights of widowhood had morphed from "happy hour" with Scott to "unhappy hours" alone. The evenings were way too long.

Filling "alone time" can be a challenge, but a strategy that does double-duty (filling time and promoting health) is to take up some form of exercise. That's easy to say but hard to commit to, especially at the end of a work day.

Get Physical

Like many physicians, Spaccarelli wants his widowed patients to be physically active. But he's also realistic. "I ask them what they like to do that's physical. That's a good place to start. Garden? Walk?" he says. And ideally the exercise should not only promote cardiovascular health but also include a flexibility regimen and walking. The important thing, he knows from his own sometimes-unfulfilled promises to exercise, is to "put it in your daily schedule, or it won't happen."

The good news is that even moderate exercise can add years to your life. In her recent book, *The First 20 Minutes: Surprising Science Reveals How We Can Exercise Better, Train Smarter, Live Longer,* Gretchen Reynolds dismisses one of the main arguments my widowed friends raise against exercising: it just takes too much time that they don't have.

In a *New York Times* interview, Reynolds explains the title of her book. "I wanted people to understand that this book is about how little exercise you can do in order to get lots and lots of health benefits. Two-thirds of Americans get no exercise at all. If one of those people gets up and moves around for 20 minutes, they are going to get a huge number of health benefits....the science shows that if you just do anything, even stand in place 20 minutes, you will be healthier."

And for those who think "no pain, no gain," she extols the value of walking, calling it "the single easiest thing anyone can do." For widows and widowers on a tight budget, it's good to hear that you don't have to invest in new shoes or fancy equipment to walk. "People have gotten the idea that exercise has to be complicated, and that they need a heart rate monitor, and a coach, and equipment and special instruction. They don't."[30]

You don't need to join a gym or walk with a partner, if finding a convenient time is just one more complication in your life. A number of websites offer downloadable exercise videos and access to online fitness communities. More and more applications are being created for use with phones and portable media players. My favorite online source of inspiration to exercise is The President's Challenge, a program that has been around since the 1960s. If you have raised children, you may remember their participation in this challenge as part of their school's physical education program.

About five years ago, my sister in Virginia invited her sisters, children, nieces, and nephews to join a subgroup of The President's Challenge, The Presidential Active Lifestyle Award (PALA) Challenge. She would take care of registering the group, enrolling participants, monitoring activity by each member, and cheering us on, all from her computer miles away from many of us. And, there were prizes, always an incentive for my competitive family: T-shirts, certificates, and even medals. Eager to join, I was off and running.

Well, mostly walking. Over the years, some of our family participants have dropped out, either because they would forget to log activities for weeks or they had found other ways to stay healthy. Not me. What I discovered about myself is not that I wanted to compete with others for prizes, but that logging hours of walking, gardening, or dancing was psychologically healthy for me. Twenty minutes of "moderate" walking earned me only ninety-two points, but each time I opened the Web page to log I realized that I had stuck to my resolve to do something active several times a week.

When the website was down a few months ago because the security system had been hacked into, I had some moments of withdrawal and near-grief: I was still exercising, but had no concrete way of recording it, no little moment of self-congratulation for sticking to my routine.

To date, I am proud to say, I have logged 541 hours and 10 minutes for a total of 130,451 points. I have ordered no T-shirts, certificates, patches, or medals to note the milestones I have completed. My reward is that I feel better physically and emotionally, just as the President's Challenge website promised. Among the reasons for staying active, the site states, is "A Sense of Well-Being: Being in good shape can give you more energy, reduce anxiety and depression, improve self-esteem, and help you better manage your stress"—all target areas for better health if you are recently widowed.

Here's the dilemma, though. Being active takes energy; but the best way to feel energetic is by being active. Psychological health and physical health are hard to separate. According to Judy Sherlock, a retired licensed clinical counselor, surviving spouses she has counseled often report intertwined physical and emotional problems during the first year or two after their spouse's death: lack of sleep, anger, depression, low energy, an "I just don't care as much as I used to" stance toward the world. They also have trouble focusing on details of life, a condition she likes to call "holes in the brain. They don't remember names, they lose keys, or they forget to pay bills."

What she assures them is that "they are just one of the unlucky ones stuck with this because of grief. Other people feel like this too." Knowing symptoms of grief that others share is particularly important, especially if you are the first of the "unlucky ones" among relatives and friends and have no one to model "normal."

Naming Grief

In a 2011 article entitled "Complicated Grief and Related Bereavement Issues for DSM-5," twenty-five physicians and scholars, led by Dr. M. Katherine Shear, argued that "complicated grief" should be included in the latest version of the *Diagnostic and Statistical Manual of Mental Disorders*, a standard reference for psychiatrists that lays out criteria for psychological conditions to help them provide appropriate treatment for patients.

To determine how persistent and acute symptoms have to be before doctors should intervene with treatment, the group set out to define "normal grief" in the first six to twelve months after the loss of a loved one. Some or all of these may describe where you are in your grief:

- Recurrent, strong feelings of yearning, wanting very much to be reunited with the person who died; possibly even a wish to die in order to be with deceased loved one;
- Pangs of deep sadness or remorse, episodes of crying or sobbing, typically interspersed with periods of respite and even positive emotions;
- Steady stream of thoughts or images of the deceased, may be vivid or even entail hallucinatory experiences of seeing or hearing deceased person;
- Struggle to accept the reality of the death, wishing to protest against it; there may be some feelings of bitterness or anger about the death;

- Somatic distress, e.g. uncontrollable sighing, digestive symptoms, loss of appetite, dry mouth, feelings of hollowness, sleep disturbance, fatigue, exhaustion or weakness, restlessness, aimless activity, difficulty initiating or maintaining organized activities, and altered sensorium [the part of the brain that processes sensory messages from the outside world];
- Feeling disconnected from the world or other people, indifferent, not interested, or irritable with others.[31]

Too bad I didn't have the benefit of this summary two months to the day after Scott died, what would have been our twenty-third wedding anniversary. It was a gloomy cold day, the day after our first Christmas without him, so I forced myself to get out of a house decorated for the holiday that held little joy for me. A walk would do me good, I convinced myself, even as I realized I would be alone with my grief and that it was sure to be a several-tissue walk as I let loose my tears.

What I really wanted was to have my husband by my side for this wintry anniversary walk. This was the first time in twenty-three years that he had not chosen a loving anniversary card for me, one decorated with images or words he knew I would "get" for their special meaning. Unlike the last twenty-two December 26ths, he had not made dinner reservations for the two of us. This walk, during which I held his image in my mind and his love in my heart, would have to suffice this year, I consoled myself.

Just then I caught sight of a Jeep rounding the corner. As it whisked by, a middle-aged driver turned and smiled at me: It was Scott. Not the pre-cancerous Scott of the thick white hair, but the one with the hair growing back after months of loss from radiation. It was Scott all right—I would know his mischievous grin anywhere.

Was it a visitation to remind me that he would always be with me? I like to think so, but I told only one person, someone I knew would believe and understand. Little did I know that I was within the range of normal grief if I experienced such "hallucinatory" sightings. I would have felt saner if I had known such experiences were not a symptom that I was going off the deep end with grief.

Over the following months, some of my intense emotional reactions began to subside as I began integrating my grief into my life; I knew I was slowly moving on. For some people, though, the intense symptoms of grief may last for years. If you feel you are stuck, not making emotional progress, you might find a counselor to map out a plan to help you get through depressing and sometimes seemingly pointless days.

According to Sherlock, behavioral red flags typically include some of these: persistently not eating, not getting out of bed, not changing your clothes—and "feeling you don't have the resources to do anything about these behaviors."

Much like someone who has suffered a brain injury, people experiencing acute grief might have to go through a "rehab" period, taking small steps, one at a time. The bereaved need to set small goals that they can accomplish, she says. One day's goal might be just to fix breakfast and feel okay about that success, knowing you can add other meals as time goes on. "Align yourself with a family member, someone to watch over your behavior," Sherlock suggests. "Tell them the promise you have made that day—to get dressed, to go for a walk—then ask them to call you so you have someone to report to." Keep trying to change behavior in little ways, she says, remembering what didn't help and what did, so you can continue any patterns that allow you to move off the plateau where you've been grounded for too long.

Short of getting professional help, you can monitor your own emotional progress by keeping track of which feelings dominate your life as the months go by. One of my college colleagues, Ken Czillinger, teaches a popular course called "Life Through Death." Much of the wisdom he shares in the course is rooted in his experience of grief after the deaths of his brother, mother, and father over a five-year period. He started some of the first support groups in Cincinnati, cofounded Parents of Murdered Children, and until recently was involved in the hospice movement.

One of the tools he has developed for helping the bereaved get in touch with their feelings is a feelings/emotions chart, too long to reproduce here with its sixty descriptive words or phrases. Because he uses it in the context of loss, the characteristics are "heavily weighted toward grief," he explains. On the list are descriptions that name where many are on their grief journey: "betrayed," "broken," "cheated," "diminished," or "forgotten," as well as at times "blessed," "courageous," "hope," "thankful," and "work finished."

Some grief experts suggest keeping a journal of your feelings, revisiting it periodically to measure whether you feel you are making any progress. That's just one of the suggestions on the website of Hamilton's Funeral Home in Des Moines, Iowa. In a list headlined "What Can I Do About My Grief?" the funeral home's Academy of Grief & Loss offers other concrete steps to regain your emotional health. Among them are these:

- Write a letter to the person who's died; tell them exactly what you're going through or resolve any "unfinished business."
- Create a safe place and go there in person or in your mind.
- Write down the loving things they said to you that you never want to forget.

- Groan in the shower. Imagine a waterfall, washing away the pain and fatigue, covering you and filling you with peace, strength and protection.
- Cry! Tears are as natural as laughter and just as healing. Tears, whether shared with others or shed in private, can help release bottled up sadness, anger, guilt, exhaustion and loneliness. *It takes a great deal more energy to keep your feelings inside than to let them out.*[32]

As you move through this hard time of regaining your physical and emotional balance, you may be somewhat consoled, as I have been, by connections with grievers of earlier generations, like Harriet Beecher Stowe, whose pain was recorded in the opening passage. We remember her for her historic book *Uncle Tom's Cabin*, but like you and me, she often felt hopeless, frozen, weary, and dead. Somehow she moved out of the space she was describing in her letter to her daughter. It takes time, but it does happen, if you take little steps, one day at a time, toward becoming whole again.

Reflection Points

- How long has it been since you've been to the doctor to assess your own health? If not since your spouse has died, make an appointment for a "well" check-up. If you have noticed any unusual physical symptoms, don't dismiss them as grief-related. Share them, and leave the diagnosis to your doctor.
- Start a feelings journal to document your movement through grief. Try to write in it at least once a week, noting the range of emotions that hit you during that day. Like physical exercise, journaling can be hard until you find your rhythm, so stick with it. Remember that the journal is only for you, so no one will be critiquing your writing. Also like

physical exercise, journaling might be the task that you skip when you get busy. Write "journal" in your calendar on specific days in a specific time slot for the coming weeks.

Role Model: Mary Kay Gilbert

For five years, Mary Kay supported her husband, Bill, through his cancer. In the weeks before his death, she was undergoing tests to determine if a lump on her breast was cancerous. Soon after the funeral, the lump was removed; the doctors assured her that they were about "99.9% sure it was benign."

They were wrong. Over the next eight months, as Mary Kay moved through radiation and two rounds of chemo, she continued working. About five years later, as her job grew more personally challenging, she remembered that her doctors had suggested that the stress of Bill's cancer could have contributed to hers. She decided to leave her job, using her free time to care for her ailing mother and to watch her niece's newborn twins.

Mary Kay continues to take care of herself, though she admits she's far from perfect. She eats more fruits and vegetables than she ever did, and feels grateful that over the years she has lost her chocoholic habits. She considers herself fortunate that tobacco or alcohol were never part of her lifestyle. Before she retired, she had a walking buddy, but now admits with a laugh that she doesn't exercise much, adding, "But I do sit on the couch and visualize myself exercising. Does that count?"

Prayer

Loving God who knows my every thought and feeling, be with me as I struggle with fatigue, "holes in my brain," and constant sadness. When I feel discouraged, help me be open to glimmers of hope and foreshadowings of healing. Bless all those who stick with me as I take little steps to keep my body and my spirit alive.

CHAPTER FIVE

Connecting and Reconnecting

For just as the body is one and has many members, and all the members of the body, though many, are one body, so it is with Christ. …But as it is, God arranged the members in the body, each one of them, as he chose. If all were a single member, where would the body be? As it is, there are many members, yet one body. The eye cannot say to the hand, "I have no need of you," nor again the head to the feet, "I have no need of you." …If one member suffers, all suffer together with it; if one member is honored, all rejoice together with it.

—1 Corinthians 12:12, 18–21, 26

MANY PEOPLE IN our culture fear death, not just their own. No matter how many bad guys they destroy playing video games, how many cities they witness being blown to bits in the movie theater, or how many tele-vised bodies they see scattered on beaches after a tsunami, they get more than a bit nervous when they can put a face on someone who has died.

Many of us surviving spouses have our unforgettable encounters with death-fearful people. The one that remains imprinted in my memory occurred in the aisle of a grocery store near my home with a man who until recently had been a neighbor, but was also a quasi-professional acquaintance of Scott's, a lawyer he'd often chat with downtown or in the courthouse.

A few days after Scott's funeral, still in a fog and dead-tired, I turned the corner with my shopping cart into the next aisle. Halfway up, I spied my ex-neighbor. His response was physical: His face contorted into a grimace, his eyes opened in horror, and he took a little leap backward, as if to escape me. I don't think he was among the five hundred or so mourners I had hugged in the reception line at Scott's wake or passed as we exited the church after the funeral. But everyone in the neighborhood and in the professional community whose life Scott had touched was aware of his illness and his death. Clearly this man was too. He stammered something, and I ended up consoling him before we parted. I pushed on thinking, "This is how it must have felt to be a leper during Jesus's day." I had something he was afraid he might catch, the leprosy of loss.

Most people don't want to be reminded of their mortality. This became clear to me during Scott's illness. Even though my colleagues knew that he had terminal brain cancer, there was still one who gingerly approached me, patted my hand, and worked up a weak smile, whispering, "I just know everything is going to be all right." And, of course, it wasn't.

These are not the kind of people you want around you as you move through your grief and try to rebuild your life. The same woman who protested that Scott surely would not die was also one who offered to help during the weeks after Scott's death. Looking back, I realize now that she had few friends and that I was in a vulnerable position to let her into my life if she would help me. Fortunately for me, one of my close, insightful friends saw what was happening and urged me to "stay away from her. She's toxic, and you don't need that now."

Happily, I had enough close family and friends around to help me through. Even though none had lost a husband, they all had experienced a death among their family or friends. They knew enough about grief not to rush me through it. And they were wise enough not to expect me to move through any "stages" in any order, at any speed.

Some laypeople and even medical professionals still cling to the notion that grief moves predictably. Recent studies have failed to support such theories, according to psychological researcher Susan Nolen-Hoeksema and therapist Judith Larson in their book *Coping with Loss*. "Many, perhaps most bereaved people do report the symptoms that stage theories describe—shock, denial, anger, despair, yearning, intrusive thoughts, and eventually a sense of recovery," they write. "But there is tremendous variability between people in the order in which these symptoms are experienced, and the duration of specific symptoms."

Because health care professionals sometimes use these stages as a guide to measure the progress of their bereaved patients, the authors go on, "people who are not following these stages might be labeled as pathological and may be intervened with unnecessarily or inappropriately." Even more troublesome is the authors' prediction that "people who read about the stages of bereavement might also label themselves as abnormal because they are not experiencing bereavement as the books say they should."[33]

An alternative to identifying stages of grieving is to reflect on characteristics that describe what your grief feels like from inside your own skin. It may be helpful as you observe your own grief to know that you are not that different from many others in your speed or style of moving through it. In *Father Loss*, a book that explores how men deal with the death of their fathers, Neil Chethik groups 376 men by their dominant style of grieving. Although the author was working with men, he admits that these characteristics may also apply to women.

About twenty percent of men interviewed for the book were

"*Dashers*...who sped through mourning; many hardly noticed it. Dashers tended not to cry, but rather to create, almost immediately, an intellectual framework to help them manage the loss…. Dashers *thought* their way through their grief."

About the same number of men in the study grieved as "Delayers" who "did not betray a powerful reaction to the death in the short-term." They experienced symptoms of mourning "months, years or even decades later—often after they had built a community of support or had come to understand themselves better."

Chethik labels another category "Displayers," who had "a powerful, acute emotional reaction" to death. "In the first few weeks after the loss, these men often felt flooded, or overwhelmed, by sadness, fear, anger, or guilt. They tended to experience their grief as happening to them; they were not in control of it."

The largest of Chethik's four groups, about forty percent of the men, were "Doers" who, even after the initial shock wore off, used action as "their primary way of processing the loss," often as a conscious way of connecting with their loved one.[34]

Reading books like Chethik's that describe grief, listening to an inspirational CD while driving, or searching for resources on the Internet are all ways you can begin to understand that there is nothing wrong with you for being despondent or feeling physically ill in the weeks or months after your loss, even if others suggest you're crying too much, or not enough, or that you should "just move on and get over it." Although you may have found a label that describes your style of mourning, still you need others to help you through your grief. Where do you find emotional support when you're experiencing shock or anger or loneliness—or all of them rolled into one?

Finding a Support Network

My five sisters were significant companions to me through the early months of widowhood, so I was surprised to read that, according to one study of 1,169 widows in the Chicago area, many bereaved are not helped much by extended kin, including siblings and relatives. In predicting results of interviews with these women sociologist Helena Z. Lopata speculated that siblings and other relatives would provide emotional support for these bereaved women.

Not so. "Siblings and relatives other than parents or children rarely appear even in the emotional support systems" of those interviewed for the study. "Only one-tenth of the listings of people to whom the widow feels closest, or to whom she would turn in times of crises, are siblings." The same holds true for social support, such as going to movies, playing cards, engaging in sports, and celebrating holidays together.

Lopata concludes that relatives outside the nuclear family rarely help widows with living costs or assist with household chores or care of children. Although other relatives, especially grandchildren, are sources of enjoyment for the widows, they offer little emotional support. In the end, her research shows, "siblings, grandparents, aunts or uncles, cousins, nieces or nephews and even grandchildren are not viable resources from which widows build their support systems."[35]

Another study of younger widows suggests that it's not who supports you but how consistently and deeply they do. The Harvard Bereavement Study included 103 widows under the age of forty-five in the first interviews, then followed smaller numbers through three weeks, eight weeks, thirteen months, and two to four years.

In their book *Recovery from Bereavement*, psychiatrist Colin Murray Parkes and sociologist Robert S. Weiss share findings based on that research, including the role others play in helping women recover after the death of a husband. What the researchers found in predicting how well the widow would recover by the beginning of the second year of loss was that the number of people supporting them, the frequency of that support, or the strength of the bond at the onset of bereavement were not that important. What mattered was the continued presence of those people as time went on.

Some of the widows in the study found it important to change their relationships with relatives and longtime friends as they moved through their grief. "Especially in the early stages of bereavement, although not so early that movement toward a new identity would itself be found to be painful, relationships with people in the same boat—other widows or widowers—could provide the understanding and matching experience necessary to fend off feelings of isolation," according to the authors.[36]

Feelings of isolation as well as physical isolation are deadly in the healing process. I remember several days after Scott's funeral rummaging through some books on tape he had borrowed, my daughters already back in school. I was overwhelmed by the sadness of being alone in the house without him. When a friend called to check on me, and assessed my state, she said, matter-of-factly, as if it should have been obvious, "Then get out of the house and go to school, even if you aren't scheduled to teach today." Being in the presence of friends lifted my spirits.

One solution to isolation, at least occasionally, is to join a therapy or counseling group of people "in the same boat." Therapists André and Susan Toth created a short-term therapy group in Buffalo, New York, to which they invited twelve women who had been widowed for between six and fourteen months, none of them exhibiting psychological issues beyond their grief.

The therapists' goal was to provide a safe environment where each woman could share her story of what it meant to be a widow. By the end of the first session, the women had formed deep bonds, like "old friends getting together after a long separation," the authors observe. "The occasion was obviously not a happy one, but the feeling of the group lacked the depressing pall it had had at first. The atmosphere was one of nervous excitement—nervous, yes, but excitement nonetheless."

One of the conversations in the group revolved around physical problems after the loss—headaches, backaches, sleeplessness. Although the group meetings did not seem to lessen those physical symptoms, many of the women reported that after the first session they had slept better than they had since their husbands had died. One woman who continued to struggle with insomnia reported to the group, "Now when I can't sleep, I know other women are going through the same thing and somehow it helps."[37]

Shared experience of loss and the belief that whatever you're feeling is "normal" seem to be the greatest benefits of support groups. When new members join the grief support group that Judy Sherlock facilitates at my parish, she asks each member, old and new, to narrate the story of the death of their loved one. "Once new members hear the others' stories, they are relieved," she observes. "A typical reaction is: 'So I'm *not* mentally ill. You sound just like me.'"

Although Sherlock has considerable expertise as a retired licensed clinical counselor who has worked with grieving individuals for years, she knows she is more valuable in the group "if I step back. I do it all the time. The more seasoned members of the group move toward healing as they help the new people in the group."

She describes three tiers of participants in the grief group: the "graduates" who are moving on, but still consider the group "family," so they occasionally visit; those who have been coming for a while but are stuck in the "this stinks" frame of mind; and the "brand new," who come regularly, many of them "angry and lost."

Although self-help support groups vary in agendas and techniques, most offer similar benefits to the bereaved, according to Therese A. Rando in her book *How to Go on Living When Someone You Love Dies.* Bereavement groups "give encouragement, provide important information and accurate norms, and transmit advice, concrete guidance, and practical suggestions for dealing with bereavement," she writes.[38]

Don't feel bad if you aren't drawn to a grief support group. I never joined one, and occasionally felt I had to "defend" my decision to those who had benefited from their experience with groups. In an article about grief on the American Association of Retired Persons website, Ruth Davis Konigsberg shares one of her "5 Surprising Truths About Grief": "You don't necessarily need counseling. Often, well-meaning friends and relatives will urge you to attend a support group, or go to see a grief counselor. Although taking such steps might make you feel better, it's certainly not a requirement for healing. According to a 2008 survey, most grief seems to go away on its own."[39]

"We Don't Cry Much…"

Because some of my friends have found relief and support in grief groups, I recently accepted an invitation to share some of my writing about grief with a group in a parish across town. The facilitator, Kathy McConnell, and I had rediscovered each other a few years earlier, each having gravitated to Cincinnati from our small hometown where we had been high school classmates. When I heard she was leading a grief group, Companions on the Journey, I didn't doubt her ability, but I wondered what the tone of the group would be: in high school she was outgoing, boisterous, and funny. How would this work with a grief group?

Very well, I discovered. Many of my preconceived notions about support groups, at least this one, were upended that evening I spent with Kathy and her group.

Arriving a bit early, I helped Kathy and her cofacilitator arrange furniture in the small meeting room off the gathering space of the church. Looking around at the comfortable chairs and the soft lighting, I asked, "Where are the tissues?"

"What do you mean?" Kathy wondered.

"For when people start to cry."

"We don't cry much, but I'll get a box if you think we should have some."

Clearly, Kathy had done her homework about grieving in her twenty years with this ministry, which began after the death of her father, an event she describes as "very hard" on her. That evening as members began trickling in, Kathy greeted them by name, setting the light tone that would permeate the meeting. After introductions, she asked everyone to "share something good that happened to you this week." Even the newest among the bereaved could pull something out of their otherwise dreary week to share.

One man had made progress in stripping the sailboat that had been sitting in his driveway, hoping to refurbish it in time for a spring maiden voyage on a nearby lake. Another, who had never traveled on her own, had mustered the courage to call an airline and book tickets for a flight to visit her deceased husband's family in Europe. Another had dug up her not-quite-thawed garden, eager to begin planting. Some were chatty and some were quiet, but all were attentive and supportive.

Kathy has learned over the years that the best "plan" for a meeting is often to throw out the plan when the group finds enthusiasm around a topic she raises. It might be a series of questions, like these she created and uses with success with every group.

"When was the last time…

- You received mail with your loved one's name on it?
- Someone spoke your loved one's name?

- You went back to a place that the two of you liked to go?
- You felt good one minute and in the pits the next minute?
- You had a really, really good day?"

Every time the group meets, their evening experience includes reflection and prayer (according to Kathy, "The only requirement for participants is that they believe in God"). At the end of this session, Kathy announced relevant events at the parish and social events for members of the group; this week it was details of where they would meet to carpool for their weekly Lenten outing to area churches' fish fries. "We're getting to be quite the connoisseurs of fish," Kathy laughed, "and a pretty snobby fish bunch at that."

Afterward, as they mingled over cake, coffee, and hot cider, a different type of sharing took place. A group clustered around a woman who had recently entered the world of online dating to hear an account of a weekend trip she had announced at a previous meeting. She had arranged to drive several hours to spend a weekend with a man she had conversed with online.

"It was bad," she shared.

"What happened?" another asked.

"It was clear early on that he was so into himself. I decided I didn't want to waste the whole weekend with him so I just left and drove home," she said, to words of affirmation from others about the rightness of that move.

By the end of the ninety minutes, there were goodbyes, hugs of affirmation, and promises to meet at 6 in the parking lot on Friday for the fish fry. Kathy had been right—no one touched a tissue.

If you decide to join a support group, it's good to research it by talking to current or past members or the facilitator, and by reading materials in print or online. One question Kathy almost always gets from bereaved men is "Are there men in the group?"

There are, as well as people who have lost children or parents, but most have lost spouses. Although many groups like Kathy's are mixed, occasionally facilitators decide to separate men from women, mainly for the sake of the men. That was a decision James Ellis made about groups he facilitates for a hospice program.

When he realized that men, especially older men, had trouble sharing feelings, he began a "covert grief group" for them, a chance to have breakfast together, sometimes inviting guest speakers, but more often slipping in "grief stuff" when it seemed helpful.

"When the older men, the World War II generation, lose their wives of decades, they are like whipped puppies," he says. "Many stay in the group for years and use it as their primary social group."

No matter when his male participants leave the group, Ellis is encouraged by signs of progress. "I've seen guys' countenances change drastically from forlorn and hesitant at first, to being able to laugh at a good joke with the other men."

A few years ago, Ellis noticed more and more younger women as hospice patients, and consequently younger widowers in need of support. Unlike their older counterparts, these men were "eager to talk about their feelings, to ask questions, and be typical mourners," he says. The age range is forty to seventy, some in their forties with children still at home to raise, but most in their upper fifties.

"Many come to this group because they have heard of men in mixed groups being set up for dates by and with the women in the group," he explains. "They often feel too vulnerable to open up in a mixed group, especially when the discussion turns to sex." Also, he has observed, if men "give in to emotions" when they're sharing about their loss, others in the all-male group don't feel uncomfortable. But, he says, most admit to saving their feelings for when they're alone.

Like other facilitators, Ellis sometimes invites present or past group members to serve as peer leaders. After working through their grief, they have gone on to lead full lives, either as single or married men, and give hope to those just beginning the journey. Although some groups require that participants move on after a designated number of years, Ellis's rule of thumb is, "They can stay as long as the group is helpful."

Moving on is what Elaine did after participating in a support group for about a year. She had joined one five months after her husband's death, a group for surviving family members of cancer patients. "It was so good!" she said. But she knew it was time to leave when "I got sick of telling my story and hearing others' sad stories."

Elaine has stayed close to several women from the group. At first, they had "the weirdest conversations. We'd describe our husbands' illnesses in great detail, and the others really wanted to listen. We'd ask each other what the funerals were like." Her husband died ten years ago, but the women still get together to have fun every few weeks.

Although I was never in a grief support group, I found a peer griever a few years after Scott died when I dated a widower for about eighteen months. Our conversations seemed like a microcosm of discussions that take place in bereavement groups in many parishes and hospice facilities.

Like Elaine and her friends, we talked in detail of our spouses' illnesses and deaths, how our children were adapting, when and why we had stopped wearing wedding rings, what we kept of our spouses' belongings after we donated everything else, and whether it was possible to fall in love after the deaths of the loves of our lives. The timing was right for these frank discussions: I was ready to process my grief then more than in the years just after Scott's death. For me, one-on-one discussion was better than any group I could have joined.

Elaine and her friends find emotional support in their female trio, but I have known larger groups that have sprung from support groups, a few men and women who really connected during sharing sessions and wanted to stay in touch. They have other friends, but these are the ones they can count on to help with home repairs, go with them to buy a car, evaluate the pros and cons of someone they're dating, share holiday meals, and volunteer together at the same booth at their annual parish festival.

Although widows and widowers may early on gravitate toward others who understand their grief, for many the need for companionship primarily with other bereaved lessens as they begin to assume an identity beyond "widow" and "widower." Most have friends who have never known the particular pain of losing a spouse, but are still part of their inner circle of friends.

Several of my widowed friends have been especially active in parish ministries, including bereavement committees, the ministries of the Eucharist and the Word, and social justice work. Some of them were invited in by a thoughtful parishioner, while others took the difficult step of going it alone to help with Giving Trees at Christmas or outreach trips to our sister parish in another state. Those first steps of transformation from being half of an involved couple to being an involved surviving spouse demand lots of courage, but often these choices lead to a wider circle of friends who share the same deep values, even if they have never known their particular deep grief.

As one of my colleagues pointed out to me soon after Scott's death, I was fortunate to have among my friends, and our friends as a couple, many single women—some of them never-married professional friends, some former religious sisters, and some active members of the religious order I had left. Fortunately, Scott and I had many close friends, single and married, that were there when I was ready to go out to a movie, share an early-morning breakfast, or commiserate about problems with children or jobs.

Without friends we would never make it through the years of grieving, not only the first year but the subsequent ones that continue to remind us of our new identity as a now-single man or woman. Our friendships are godsends, new ones forged in the fire of widowhood and old ones, a place of comfort and familiarity as we acclimate to a new life.

As you connect and reconnect during your grief, you might come to better understand that each of us has a role in building up this Body of Christ so central to our religious belief. In the beginning of the grief process, you may be the eyes, streaming tears, or the lips, verbalizing your grief. But as time goes on, even without noticing it, you may shift to new roles, realizing that "if one member suffers, all suffer together with it."

Soon you may be for others the eyes that see pain too deep to speak, or the ears that listen to a story too sad for others to bear to hear, or the arms that reach out to embrace those who need you as a promise that they will eventually make it through this experience, like St. Paul, "afflicted in every way, but not crushed; perplexed, but not driven to despair."

Reflection Points

• If it feels right, check out some support groups available through your parish or ones that others recommend, on the online community resource page of the funeral home that handled your spouse's service, or the website www.griefshare.com. Do some research, find one you like, and, if you don't feel brave enough to go alone, invite a friend or relative to accompany you on this maiden voyage. Remember that one visit does not commit you to stay with that group.

• Have you received offers of "Let's do something some time" from a friend or relative? Now might be that "some time." E-mail or call to take them up on their offer, but be sure you have input on what feels right at this time and how long you want to be away from home.

Role Model: Judy Sherlock

When her husband died, Judy Sherlock, sixty-six, realized that like others who are newly bereaved, she had some grief work to do: after forty-five years as a wife, she had lost her identity. She continues to work on her own journey of transformation through prayer and meditation. But as an experienced counselor, she also reaches out to others in her parish. Like Naomi in the book of Ruth, she leads members of the parish grief support group back to their "homeland," a place of peace, helping them be open to the subtle encounters with grace that will allow them to once again fully participate in life.

Prayer

Creative God, allow me to be open to the graces that infuse this time of sadness in my life: friends and relatives who understand that there is no timeline for healing, volunteers and professionals who bring their energy and experience to support groups where I can feel normal in my grief, the varied members of the Body of Christ who, believing that "if one member suffers, all suffer together with it," hold me and other bereaved in their hearts and prayers.

CHAPTER SIX

Helping Children Through the Hurt

"Dad, Wavey says I have to ask you. I want to go to the awake for Uncle Jack."…

"Bunny it's 'the wake,' not 'the awake.'… Let me talk to Wavey about this."

But Wavey thought it was right for them to go.

Quoyle said there had been too much death in the past year.

"But everything dies," said Wavey. "There is grief and loss in life. They need to understand that. They seem to think death is just sleep."

Well, said Quoyle, they were children. Children should be protected from knowledge of death. And what about Bunny's nightmares? Might get worse.

"But, m'dear, if they don't know what death is how can they understand the deep part of life? The seasons and nature and creation—"[40]

— E. Annie Proulx, *The Shipping News*

QUOYLE, THE SINGLE father in Annie Proulx's novel *The Shipping News*, had done the best he could after his wife died in a car wreck, even reading the book the funeral director had supplied, *A Child's Introduction to Departure of a Loved One*. But his efforts to protect his two daughters from the reality of their mother's death were backfiring; his biggest mistake—telling them that their mother was not "dead," just asleep in heaven.

As you are dealing with your grief—practical decisions, as well as the spiritual, physical, and emotional ramifications of your spouse's death for your own life—you may have children who are on a parallel but highly personal journey through their own grief. Being attentive to their needs immediately after the funeral and through the first years is one of the most important challenges newly widowed parents face.

According to J. William Worden, "...for the great majority of children, parents remain their most significant others; in effect, their partners in negotiating the essential developmental tasks that will take them to adulthood. The loss of a parent to death and its consequences in the home and in the family change the very core of the child's existence."

In his book *Children and Grief: When a Parent Dies,* Worden shares findings from the Harvard Child Bereavement Study that he codirects. He identifies four "tasks of mourning" children must perform to recover from the trauma of a parent's death. The first is "to accept the reality of the loss."[41] How a parent communicates this and how the child hears it will vary according to the circumstances of the death and the age of the child.

During Scott's illness I tried to prepare my daughters, then eighteen, fifteen, and thirteen, for the possibility of his death. They knew that he would eventually die, but always wanted me to pinpoint the date of death, for example, wondering if he would be alive at Christmas. Of the three, my middle daughter, Liz, was most in denial, even after her father was admitted to the intensive care unit. One evening that week, she asked, "Will Dad be home in time for Halloween?" I have no doubt that she began accepting the reality when I replied. "I don't think he will be coming home from the hospital...ever."

As harsh as the answer seemed at that time, I was glad a few days later that I hadn't sidestepped the difficult question. When we decided to take Scott off life support, several sisters volunteered to gather family and friends for a bedside farewell; I knew that I had to go myself to Liz's school to tell her the news. The school staff had arranged for us to meet in the nurse's room, which would be more private than the school office. When I told her we needed to go to the hospital to say good-bye to her father, her response was direct and honest: "If I could see God right now, I'd slap him in the face." The reality had set in, and she was confronting it.

Although Liz was the last of my daughters to accept the grim reality, once she did, she faced it head-on. At Scott's bedside after the songs and prayers of family and friends, she was the first to accept my invitation to "say good-bye to Dad now, and be sure you say it loud so he can hear you."

"Daddy," Liz almost shouted, "I love you!" then looked alarmed as she saw tears streaming out of Scott's closed eyes: "I've made him sad."

"No you haven't, honey," I assured her. "Those are tears of happiness because he knows you love him."

Because my children had been through the death of their grandmother when they were younger, they had some grasp of the finality of death. Helping younger children accept this reality may be a process rather than a one-time conversation. It may mean repeating the message, whatever form that takes, even as children are moving through Worden's second task: "to experience the pain and emotional aspects of the loss."

The pain and emotions will vary according to the age and personality of the child, according to Peg Lynch, who coordinates bereavement groups for a hospice program. "It's critical to know where your children are developmentally. Meet them where they are," she advises. "Try opening conversations with 'Tell me about what's happening inside you and how you're feeling.'"

It wasn't until six months after his wife died that Tom realized he was so wrapped up in his own grief that he hadn't been paying enough attentions to his son's. "I could see that Nick, nine at the time, was being eaten up with grief. He'd say something and I wasn't catching his signals when he wanted to talk," Tom remembers. "He'd say, 'Well, Dad, Mom did it this way,' and it took me a while to realize that was the signal to drop everything."

His advice to grieving parents: "When your kids are ready to share something in their hearts, listen. You have to let your own grief go to the side in that moment. If you're bawling your eyes out and your kid asks you a question, you have to stop right then and listen. If you don't, they'll think you don't care and that you won't be there to support them in this very hard thing they're going through."

Pay Attention to the Signs

According to Lynch, children may express their pain at the loss in a variety of forms. Physical changes may include uncontrollable crying, changes in eating patterns, hypersensitivity to noise, fatigue, and bodily aches and pains that they can't exactly pinpoint.

She also says that how children think about the death may vary. Older children sometimes feel guilty or blame themselves for it. Insecurity and fear may also dominate the thoughts of children at any age. They worry about how the family will exist without their dead parent and fear that the pain they are immersed in will go on forever.

One of the most common fears widowed parents note is their children's anxiety about the death of the surviving parent. My youngest, Annie, would regularly remind me to drive carefully as I was leaving the house. Fortunately, my only car accident occurred about ten years after

Scott's death, but even then it was traumatic for all my daughters. On my way to a morning class, I pulled through an intersection at a green light, and luckily out of the corner of my eye, I saw a car running the red light. I slammed on my brakes so that the oncoming driver collided with my left front fender rather than directly into the driver's door.

Still the damage was serious enough that I arrived at the emergency room of a local hospital in an ambulance. And my car was totaled. When Annie arrived in the ER, she was shaken but relieved enough that she was able to chat and even joke with a friend who had left work to be with me. It was Annie's task to drive to the lot where my car had been towed to retrieve my books, computer, and other personal items. Later she told me that it was only when she saw the car that the danger I had been in hit her: She began shaking and crying at the thought that she might have lost her only parent.

That fear never goes away for my children. Later the day of the accident, Liz arrived from her job an hour away to be with me at home. Her teary words when she arrived summarized that fear so well: "I'm mad, I'm sad, I'm scared."

This overwhelming worry about parents is just one of the emotional reactions Lynch hears from children in the grief support groups she facilitates. Others include moodiness, sadness, relief (if the dead parent had been abusive), defiance, hostility against the surviving parent, irritability, and a sense of abandonment.

When Cheryl's husband, Mark, died, she thought she had prepared her two children, Brady, six, and Blake, three, during their father's eighteen-month battle with lung cancer. "At first I explained that he had a terrible disease and that he was really sick," she remembers. "I told them that we were doing everything we could to get their dad better. When things started going downhill, I had several talks with them about how sometimes the body doesn't respond to medicine and even though their dad wanted to get better we were not sure it was going to happen."

After Mark's death, Cheryl knew that helping her children would be a challenge because she had witnessed "the emotional roller coaster" her brother's children had gone through when he had died. "It was very difficult for me to explain to my two children why this happened and what death was when I couldn't understand myself how this had happened."

Like many parents in her situation she turned to those more experienced with grief for help. She remembers Fernside, a center for grieving children, as "a life saver for me and my children." Cheryl and her boys went through the program twice, once after Mark died and three years later. She was learning that children's understanding of death changes as they mature. Psychologists tell us that most children do not understand that death is permanent until at least age seven.

Cheryl says that her experiences at Fernside "allowed me to connect with other parents who were going through the same thing while my children were able to connect with fellow children who had lost a parent. Brady once told me that the program made him feel better since at school none of his friends knew what he was going through. The program really helped the boys express their feelings in a safe manner."

At times grief leads to changes in behavior, some of them unsafe, according to Lynch. Younger children may regress to earlier habits, such as thumb-sucking. Some children withdraw and become lethargic, while others become overactive or aggressive. Older children may get involved with risky behaviors, such as alcohol or drug abuse. She also observes that many times children's performance in school declines.

Soon after the death of Tom's wife, he realized that one of the practical details he would have to take care of was alerting their schools that his sons had lost their mother. He went to both schools to suggest what they might do to help and made it a point to take time off work as often as he could to be with them for important events.

When Angie's husband, Gerry, died after a three-month illness, only two of her children were still in school. She worried about her third child, Lauren, who was about to begin college, a new place where she would not have many of her friends to support her. The hospice chaplain took it upon herself to call the campus ministers at the college to ask them to keep an eye out for Lauren during her first weeks there.

Fortunately Angie's youngest child, Tim, was just starting eighth grade in a familiar school at the time of Gerry's death. In addition to Fernside, he found peers in a grief group the school psychologist started because four children in the school had recently lost parents. "All the teachers in the school were supportive and couldn't have been more helpful," Angie remembers.

Not so with one particular teacher in my daughter Annie's middle school. Intelligent, but never a stellar student, Annie was distracted by her father's illness and death the first few months in this school she had recently transferred to as an eighth-grader. Math was particularly challenging because she was having trouble focusing.

I'm not sure Annie had ever witnessed such explosive anger from her usually calm mother the day she came home from school and reported that her math teacher had called her out in the hall to tell her, "Annie, it's been three weeks since your Dad died. It's time you get over it and start paying attention so you can pass this class."

Within minutes I was in my car speeding to the school to talk to the psychologist who had been helpful during Scott's illness and after his death. He was as appalled as I was at the comment so he arranged for a counselor from Cancer Family Care to meet with Annie's teachers to help them understand what she was going through and how it might affect her work.

Adjusting to New Routines

School routines may call for adjustments in family roles, for example if the deceased mother was active in extracurricular events or a father regularly monitored homework. The real adjustments, however, occur in the home, where empty chairs at the dinner table or mail addressed to the deceased continually remind children that their family will never be the same. Even while they're working through the emotional pain of loss, children begin to face Worden's third task of mourning: "to adjust to an environment in which the deceased is missing."

Older children may leap to some false conclusions about what the reconfigured family might look like, as was the case when teenaged Tim announced to his mother shortly after his father's funeral, "I guess we don't need to sit down to eat dinner anymore." Wanting to get this attitude cleared up immediately, Angie responded, "Of course we do, we're still a family."

In a scholarship essay Tim wrote, "Overcoming Adversity," he reflects, "I knew that I was going to have to work hard to overcome what had happened to me as I had lost both my close male role models. My dad had passed away, and my older brother had to move out of town for work. This meant I had to be the man of the house for my mom, and I was not even out of junior high."

Several years after Gerry's death when Angie read the essay she felt bad that Tim had felt he had to step into his father's shoes. Looking back on the first Christmas without Gerry, she remembers Tim saying, "We'll never have a Christmas tree because we won't be able to do it without Dad." She assured him that if they couldn't handle it, they would get help from other adult friends.

A family friend, Mike, became the "go-to friend" for challenges like Christmas trees. As one of Gerry's best friends, he vowed to attend every soccer game Tim played throughout high school. "And he did, even the games out of town," says Angie. "It touched my heart. I don't know if Gerry would have gone to as many because he wasn't into sports."

Like Angie, Tom had to celebrate holidays without a spouse. Some holidays were hard to recreate without Sue, who had been a whiz at sewing and a creative decorator. Soon after Sue's death on December 14, Tom remembers, "We got up on a Sunday and I thought, 'Oh my God, we've got Christmas to deal with.'" They had a "tiny tree" that year. The holiday was brightened a bit when Tom and his two young sons were treated to an evening celebration with a neighbor who came over to their house dressed as Santa.

During the first year of adjustment to life without his wife, Tom's "mantra was 'What Would Sue Do?'" Sue had worked full-time, but having studied fashion design, she always found time to sew. A few months after her death, Tom went to the basement, pulled out one of the patterns stored there, opened her machine, and began to teach himself to sew.

When his curious sons came down to join him and asked, "Dad, what are you doing?" he told them, "This is how Mom did it." Although he never actually finished the shirt he had started, his sewing sprees became occasions for family parties: the boys sitting in pajamas their mother had made, eating snacks while their father negotiated the finer details of his newly learned craft. Those gatherings of the "new" family were healing, he says. "It was almost as if Sue was with us in the basement."

As children progress through developmental stages, the death of a parent often moves back into their consciousness to remind them in fresh ways of their loss, just as they think they're finally adjusting. Among the most difficult occasions, according to my friends, are graduations, weddings, and births of grandchildren.

When Annie graduated from high school, after the family had survived her three hospitalizations for depression, cutting, and an eating disorder, we knew her graduation was a big deal, even if she was just one name on the printed program. She had received no awards, no honors, no letters or plaques for extracurricular achievements, no mention of scholarships to colleges—we were just happy she was alive and had made it to this day.

After hugs and roses from her two older sisters, the four of us piled into my car, opened the sunroof and blasted the sound track from the movie *Pretty Woman* as we drove to a favorite restaurant. Over pizza, we reminisced with her friends about childhood experiences and told funny stories about Scott, who was not with us physically but was certainly there in spirit.

Angie's oldest son Matt was married eleven months after Gerry died. She remembers how she kept trying to "hold it together at the wedding and the reception. During the traditional groom-mother dance, we didn't dance, but just stood on the dance floor, crying together."

As the mother of three brides, I faced the emotional challenge of being there with my daughters even as they were missing their father. New family traditions began with Katie's wedding, when she asked me if I would walk her down the aisle. To publicly acknowledge her absent father, she had asked each of his two brothers to carry in a sunflower, a flower that had become important during his illness as a sign of hope, a spray of which had topped his casket. Her two sisters followed her lead a few years later, so my presence at their sides and their uncles preceding us down the aisle has become an important memory for us and our families.

Not long after the first wedding, the grandchildren started arriving. When I realize that they will never know a Grandpa Barkley, I take comfort in remembering that Katie was the only of my daughters alive when Scott's father, the first Grandpa Barkley, died. Katie and Scott's dad, separated in age by half a century, were great reading buddies, as pictures in our album attest.

Katie took her first steps in the funeral home at his wake, but of course she has no memory of him. Still he was part of the fabric of our lives through our pictures and stories their father and uncles told over the years. No paternal grandfather—still my daughters turned out okay, I console myself as each new grandchild arrives.

For Angie's family, connection between her grandchildren and a grandfather they never knew is kept alive through pictures of Gerry in her house. She was delighted by a recent comment from her six-year-old granddaughter as she was looking at one of them: "Grandpa in Heaven is a really nice name."

Angie's family's connection to a deceased father and grandfather is one way of addressing Worden's fourth task of mourning: "to relocate the dead person within one's life and find ways to memorialize the person." Soon after death, the connection might be a physical one, through a "transitional" or "linking object."

The day Cheryl's husband died, two girls from the parish school delivered Angel Bears for each boy, "a stuffed bear that they had sewn wings onto. My boys have loved them ever since. I had placed them in the casket in Mark's arms during the layout. The boys knew that was the last thing that their dad hugged so whenever they get sad and miss their dad, they go grab their daddy bears."

For my youngest our family dog was a connection to her father. She remembers, "I found great solace in our family dog, Kalby. She was 'Dad's dog' so I always knew a special part of him was with her. It was difficult when Kalby died because it felt like that piece of Dad was gone for good."

As children mature, they find new ways to relate to and remember the deceased. Although Tim's father was never a sports fan and Tim ended up with ten varsity sports letters, a belated connection came in the form of birdhouses. A pack rat by Angie's description, Gerry had parts of birdhouses all over the basement, which she often nagged him to clean out. Recently Tim surprised her with a gift that connected them both to Gerry. Having found pieces to a birdhouse, Tim assembled and finished it, presenting it to her for Christmas.

Both Angie's family and mine have participated in an annual Run to Remember over the years, organized by the family of a deceased woman who had loved to run. Annie saw an announcement of the run on a park home page and signed us up, adding Scott's name to the list of other deceased honorees—a good way to remember Scott but also an effective way to contribute to the community. Proceeds each year allow the park to add equipment to an inclusive park, "where all children, with and without disabilities, can play and learn together in a healthy recreational environment."

Another way we found to memorialize Scott was to tap into our image of him as a man who had served in Vietnam but who hated war and violence, the effects of which he saw often during his years as a television news photographer. When I was pregnant with Liz, he had been on a trip to Beirut, narrowly avoiding death the morning a suicide bomber blew up the U.S. Marine compound there in 1983, killing 241 marines and fifty-eight French soldiers.

After Scott's death, when a group initiated a campaign to erect a peace pole in a local park, we were eager to learn details. The design, described on the sponsoring group's website, convinced us this was a perfect match for Scott's values: "A nine-foot, hexagonal, granite pole [is] surrounded by six granite benches. Each bench is six-foot in length and has two translations of the phrase May Peace Prevail on Earth. The inscribed languages are Arabic, Cherokee, Chinese, English, French, German, Hebrew, Hindi, Japanese, Russian, Spanish and Swahili." The paver we purchased is a permanent memory to my daughters of their father's life, inscribed with the words, "Scott Barkley, man of peace."

Although these memories are now happily recalled amid tears, the first years of loss often challenge a parent to deal with tears, their own and their grieving children's, with little immediate relief. Like Cheryl, you may find that you need to recalibrate and seek additional help as your children mature. And life events challenge even adult children to revisit and deal with their loss and sadness. Most support groups define no time limits for participation in healing activities.

My area is fortunate enough to have Fernside as a permanent resource for grieving children. The second oldest children's grief center in the nation, it was modeled after the Dougy Center in Portland, Oregon, which has a strong presence on the web, allowing families all over the world to tap into the center's accumulated wisdom and resources. The site offers helpful advice, such as "Answer the questions they ask. Even the hard ones," "Talk about and remember the person who died," and "Take a break: Children grieve in cycles. Having fun or laughing is not disrespectful to the person who died; this is a vital part of grieving too."

On a page about teens and grief, you will read that, "In our work with teenagers, we've learned that teens respond better to adults who choose to be companions on the grief journey rather than direct it. We have also discovered that adult companions need to be aware of their own grief issues and journeys because their experiences and beliefs impact the way they relate to teens."

An activities page for children provides a "Finish the sentences" exercise, prompting children to complete lines such as "The thing that makes me saddest is…," "One thing I liked to do with the person who died is…," "Since the death my friends…." There's even an online support group link, "Inspire," which "connects teens, young adults, and their families who are grieving a death for support and inspiration."

Even if your teens access online support, hospice coordinator Lynch reminds parents that after a death it is "critical to keep communication open. They should have at least three 'go-to adults' they can process their feelings with." For older children, that may be an aunt or uncle, a teacher or a coach. "You should not feel jealous of the other adults, as long as your kids are talking to someone good," she says. "Your older children will eventually talk to you as long as you're open and let them know 'I'm here when you're ready to talk.'"

Helping children through grief may be one of the most difficult challenges you face as a grieving spouse, as you try to supply what Worden explains they need most after a parent dies: "support, nurturance, and continuity." You are not in this alone, as Angie discovered when Mike stepped up with an offer to attend all her son's soccer games or when Cheryl twice found a safe place for her two sons at Fernside.

Particularly if you're parenting bereaved teens, it may be years before you know the impact you have had during this scary time in their lives. One of my rewards came two years after Scott's death when Katie shared with me a copy of a talk she had given on a college retreat. Opening with memories of the familiar struggle between a teenage daughter and her mother, she went on to describe learning about Scott's cancer diagnosis and traveling home from camp with an aunt to be with us. She wrote:

> At this time in my life, when my dad got sick, God made Himself SO present in my life that I couldn't ignore it anymore. He spoke so loudly and clearly to me that I was forced to listen and I couldn't help but respond. And it was through my mom

that He did this. When I got out of my aunt's Toyota after the hour drive home from camp and walked up my driveway and into my dimly lit house and fell into the arms of my mother, I fell into God's open arms. I felt surrounded by warmth and energy in my mother's arms. As my mom wrapped me in her arms, and without speaking, assured me that I would be okay, God scooped me up from my place of darkness and brought me into the light of his loving arms. And from that point, that emotional, terrifying, exhausting moment, He never let me go.

Reflection Points

• If friends or relatives ask how they can help you help your children, ask them to order books or DVDs for the family from the Dougy Center website: http://www.dougy.org/.

• When you and your children feel ready, plan a dinner that their deceased mom or dad would have liked. Put aside concerns about healthy eating, and go with whatever they suggest. Then shop, prepare, and eat it as a family.

Role Model: Joe Biden

Joe Biden had just been elected to the United States Senate when his wife and little girl were killed in a car accident and his two young sons were hospitalized with broken bones and head injuries. In his memoir *Promises to Keep: On Life and Politics*, Biden writes, "Except for the memorial service, I stayed in the hospital room with my sons. My life collapsed into their needs. If I could focus on what they needed minute by minute, I thought I might stay out of the black hole."

In a new job in a new place without his wife, he adjusted to life in the Senate by day, and returned home to Delaware at night to put his sons to bed. He was helped through his grief by remembering the "first principle of life" he had learned from his father: "Get up! The art of living is simply getting up after you've been knocked down."[42]

Prayer

Loving God, you are immense enough to be father and mother to us all. Give me the grace to be the best grieving parent I can be, a role model in dealing with my grief while tending to my children's. Help me to listen to, embrace, affirm, and unconditionally love my children as they move through the forever-changed rhythms of our family life.

CHAPTER SEVEN

Losing an Intimate Confidant

The widow looks in the mirror
thinking, no one will ever touch
me again, never. Not hold me.
Not caress the softness of my
breasts, my inner thighs, the swell
of my belly. Do I still live
if no one knows my body?[43]

    —Marge Piercy, "The Tao of Touch"

IT WAS A few months after Scott's death. Still recovering from the physical demands of his illness and dreading the intense workload of the end of a college semester with Christmas lurking around the corner, I mustered up some energy to head to a nearby mall. Just as I had neglected my physical health over the past six months, I had also ignored the shabby underwear that lined my dresser drawers. Clearly, I needed to replenish.

It was the end of the day. The lingerie department was crowded, the artificial light too intense for my somber mood. Half-heartedly, I rummaged through the endless choices of bras in my size and my style. Then it caught my eye: a bra, my size, embroidered with just enough lace to be sexy yet comfortable. Suddenly, I was face-to-face with a bleak future without the joyful intimacy that had marked my marriage to

Scott. In what must have looked like a moment of melodrama to nearby shoppers, I tearfully collapsed on the floor under a rack of bras. Who would care what my new bra looked like? Who would ever see it but me? I wasn't grieving a future life without sex; I was grieving the loss of daily intimacy and awakening touch. My tomorrows would be without warm hugs, quick kisses as we each sped out the door on our way to work, on-the-go phone calls to check on each other and the kids ("I just called to say I love you"), cryptic notes on corners of yellow television news scripts left underneath my car's windshield wiper ("I love you XX"). Mostly, though, I was mourning the loss of our cozy debriefings at the end of the day, when we shared insights and complaints about our children, our jobs, our world.

Other widows point to similar voids in their lives. One whose husband's death had been sudden and unanticipated told me that for a while after his death she would make a mental note to "tell John about that" before she realized that there would no longer be a John joining her at the dinner table when she arrived home.

How you cope with your own physical and emotional needs without your spouse will depend on a variety of factors: the quality of life you experienced in your marriage, other support systems that can partially fill the void of a lost confidant, and your desire to date and possibly remarry.

In the book *Perspectives on Bereavement*, Tamara Ferguson shares some research about "How Young Widows Have Coped with Their Problems." She reports "one-quarter of the widows said that loneliness was their most serious problem. They missed the companionship of their husbands and talking over daily events, and felt especially lonely in the evenings and weekends."

This desire for companionship is not limited to young widows. A case in point is my father, Wally. Widowed at age seventy-eight after a fifty-six year marriage, he sought new friends in a senior citizen dance group. Searching for companionship, not love, he took several women out for dinner and dancing.

Interested in attending the next dance, but knowing few of the dancers, he overheard Vera, whom he had danced with once at an event, saying she might not attend because she didn't have a ride. Always a gentleman, Wally offered to pick her up and take her home if she would save the first and last dance for him. Vera hadn't dated since the death of her dancer-husband, but she thought it over for a few days and took Wally up on his offer. Frankly, he says, he was surprised that she called. "We started very casually as companions to do things together," he says. "We were shocked when we realized how important we were becoming to each other, how one of us starts to say exactly what the other was thinking, and how we have helped each other lead a fulfilling existence."

Many surviving spouses find confidants among family and friends. In a 2008 article in the *Journal of Marriage and Family*, Jung-Hwa Ha examines widows' and widowers' "confidant relationship," which she describes as "a relationship in which one can share private feelings" that "has a positive effect on one's morale and health."

For many married persons, especially men, a spouse is among the most important confidants. "Thus, losing a spouse," writes Ha, "can have a detrimental effect on one's available social support, particularly if the surviving spouse has depended primarily, if not solely, on her/his spouse for emotional support prior to widowhood." The study revealed that about six months after the loss, "there is a rallying of support around surviving spouses, and family and friends are sensitive to the needs of the bereaved spouse." As time passes, however, this support does not seem an adequate substitute for the loss of the spouse who had provided emotional support.

The study also found that at the six-month point of bereavement the widowed receive great emotional support from children, but that as time goes on "older widowed parents may not need as much support from children as they needed at the initial stage, and children may also perceive that their parents do not need as much support.... Another possibility is that children cannot maintain a high commitment to their widowed parents' emotional needs over time."[44]

In addition to depriving a widow or widower of someone with whom to share daily details of life, the death of a spouse presents another unmet need: what poet Marge Piercy calls "the tao of touch." In the final stanza of the poem by that name, Piercy summarizes the universality and indispensability of touch to humans:

> We touch each other so many
> ways, in curiosity, in anger,
> to command attention, to soothe,
> to quiet, to rouse, to cure.
> Touch is our first language
> and often, our last as the breath
> ebbs and a hand closes our eyes.[45]

Loss of touch for me in the first years of widowhood was most acute at night, in the loneliness of my now half-empty bed. Like many other couples, as our marriage matured we engaged in sexual intercourse less frequently than in our early marriage, but we were still intimate.

An Absence of Touch

A 1999 study conducted by the American Association of Retired Persons and *Modern Maturity* magazine surveyed 1,384 men and women over the age of forty-five to gather information about sexual attitudes and behaviors. Participants responded that within the past six months, 43 percent of males and 35 percent of females had engaged in sexual intercourse once a week or more often. Other forms of intimacy were reported at a higher level: 74 percent of men and 48 percent of women hugged or kissed at least once or more a week; 63 percent of men and 47 percent of women sexually touched or caressed their spouse at least once or more a week.[46]

Of all the physical contact Scott and I shared, what I missed most after his death was the nighttime body-to-body comfort, usually my back snuggling into the contour of his front, his arms around me in a nighttime embrace. Suddenly single, there was no way to replicate this intimate and soothing position.

But that does not mean my life was devoid of touch. As often as I could, I lovingly hugged my daughters in mutual efforts to provide physical comfort. Once grandchildren arrived, I luxuriated in cuddling with newborns that needed comfort to get back to sleep (sometimes ignoring my daughter's admonition to "not pick her up, just let her cry herself back to sleep").

And I found another source of comforting touch right in my own house: our family's Australian shepherd, Kalby. She was the dog I had protested getting when Scott suggested we find another dog a year after the death of our eighteen-year-old dachshund, Bark. I loved dogs, but now was not the right time: We were both working, we had three young children, and I was just beginning doctoral studies.

But Scott was nothing if not persistent. He returned from a foray among the stacks at our library with a pile of books, including one about choosing the right pet for a family with young children. He narrowed it down to about five breeds that looked like a good fit, then began to break down my resolve. Finally, I agreed, but not to "a big hairy dog that will make vacuuming even harder." A week later, he set up a projector and screen in our family room for a full slide show starring a friend's big, hairy Aussie. We were hooked.

During Scott's illness, Kalby never left his side, whether he was in bed or sitting on the front porch. Unstable on his feet after surgery, Scott wobbled away from a chair, about to tumble, and Kalby lunged to break the fall. After Scott's death, she stopped sleeping in our bedroom, plopping herself right inside the front door, perhaps waiting for him to return, more likely knowing that a household of four women now needed extra security.

She was furry, and she was soft. The girls especially loved to rub her ears, joking about which of the three would get an ear as a souvenir when Kalby died. In the years after Scott's death she was not only a companion (and a motivation to keep in shape on our daily walks) but also a source of comforting touch. She would snuggle up to me on the couch as I read, and I would find comfort in stroking her soft fur and rubbing her ears. Kalby could not bring Scott back to me, but she was a source of connection and healing touch.

To Date or Not to Date

But there is another option for meeting intimacy needs. Many discussions about intimacy among the widowed weigh in on the pros and cons of dating. Since I never participated in a grief support group, where the topic of dating typically arises, I had given little consideration to that possibility in the first few years after Scott's death. I was too concerned with getting control over finances, my children's healing and education, and practical matters, such as dealing with a domino effect of broken-down appliances and cars that needed repair or replacement.

Before his death, Scott and I had talked about my remarriage. "I want you to date and get married again, if you find someone right for you," he had told me. "You're young, smart, and attractive, so it shouldn't be hard." When I had my first date, I was glad that I could repeat his words to my youngest daughter, who greeted my casual announcement of the date with "Dad would be so ticked at you."

The date was not my idea. A friend of many years announced that she and her husband had decided, "It's time for you to date. We have just the guy." The guy was her brother-in-law who had been widowed several years before Scott's death. I was up for it, but had little experience to fall back on. Having joined the convent six days after turning seventeen, I knew little about the dating scene. I was essentially a one-man woman.

More of my male than female widowed friends are open to dating and marriage, often fairly soon after the loss of a spouse. As one male grief counselor noted to me, "Men don't do alone well."

Fifty-one-year-old Tom H. says that "most of the guys in my grief group are dating someone." It wasn't until recently, almost two years after his wife's death, that he had any desire to date.

Right now, he says, raising three children ages fifteen, thirteen, and eleven after his wife's unexpected death is about all he can handle. "To start a relationship now wouldn't be fair to my kids or the woman I would be dating." He's not "actively seeking anyone right now" but admits that "if the right person came along, well maybe."

Tom's interest in dating is pretty typical of attitudes uncovered in several research projects. One study of men and women sixty-five and older published by Deborah Carr in the *Journal of Marriage and Family* in 2004 reiterates what many widows know without any research: there are more women than men among the bereaved. Because women generally live longer than men, women ages sixty-five and older outnumber men by about three to two. So, should men wish to date there are more opportunities. And the wisdom on the widowed streets is quite clear: widowed men are usually interested in younger women.[47]

Scant availability of men is not the only reason widows don't date. In a 1998 article in the *Journal of Aging Studies*, Maria M. Talbott shares some typical responses from older widows she interviewed, trying to uncover attitudes toward remarriage. Among reasons they're not interested in dating and remarriage:

- "I don't want another man: They're a plague of nuisance."
- "I like having a man around the house, but I'm not willing to acquire another one and break him into my way of thinking."
- "For the first time in my life, I have no responsibilities except for myself.... In other words, I'm just learning to fly a little bit. And I love it."[48]

Mary Kay, widowed after twenty-eight years of marriage, articulates a typical reason my widowed friends give for not dating. "Yes, I'm lonely and I don't like it. The world is made for couples," she says. Still she has never even considered dating. "What I had with Bill was so special. I would compare everyone to Bill. No one would be able to love me like him. Everyone would pale next to him," she says.

Before Jane's children were all in college, she never considered dating. In 2005, she met a man through a Catholic singles Internet dating service whose site tagline was "Is your Catholic faith important to you? Don't be Fooled by Others...Join a True Catholic Community!" Her faith was important to her, so she gave it a try.

She was excited when she met a man from several states away and ended up dating him for two years, getting together with him about every two months. But the long-distance nature of the relationship was not the reason they ended it. "Thank goodness he broke it off," she says.

"I loved him very much, and thought we'd be able to work around the deep differences in our political leanings. He was a daily fan of conservative radio talk shows, and I was molded by my mother's sense of social justice—we were never able to reconcile these."

Despite their differences, breaking up wasn't easy for Jane. "We could talk. He was smart and made life fun for me," she says. "It took a while for me to get over him." She never returned to that dating website, but did date three other men, all retired. Although she got along "extremely well" with the first one, she found herself exhausted from spending every weekend with him after her intense week at work. "He didn't have a life. I was his life," she says. "And he got way too serious way too fast after coming off a divorce. We broke up after about six months, and only then did I find out that he had already bought an engagement ring for me."

Jane met the man she's presently dating, a retired Presbyterian minister, on another dating website. Widowed two years ago, he has much to offer her, including strong communication skills so she can share openly how she feels with him, especially about being pressured to move toward marriage too quickly. "I'm attracted to men who are trusting and good. I'd like to marry some day but I want to be positive that we have common interests," Jane says. "I know too many people who jumped into marriage too quickly and they are very unhappy."

Rick, who was sixty when his wife of thirty-four years died, felt the desire to date about five months after her death, explaining that he "felt a void without female companionship. I missed going out, holding hands, seeing a movie with a woman." At first he started dating for companionship, meeting women for coffee or meals. Often he had two or three dates, but sometimes the relationship lasted for up to eight dates. Over twenty months he met sixty women, almost all of them over the Internet. So he knows the challenges of Web dating: "People only tell you what they want to tell you about themselves."

Social networking, especially via Facebook and Twitter, has changed the way in which many widows and widowers today get to know people before they meet in person. It's difficult to really know a potential date without meeting them, Rick cautions. After about three hours face-to-face with one woman who had shared a lot with him over social media, he knew the relationship would go nowhere. When he ended it, the woman felt spurned. She hacked into his Facebook account, posing as Rick, and posted some offensive messages to his female friends. Rick had to change his password and hire an attorney to get rid of her.

He met Patti, the woman he eventually married, through his cousin, who had known her since childhood. Even before he and his future wife met in person, he talked to her a lot, the old-fashioned way, over the phone. "Our marriage runs smoothly because we talk a lot about things and respect each other's spaces," Rick says, advising, "Before you make the decision to marry, you need to spend a couple hundred hours talking, about everything."

Rick dated enough women before Patti that he felt competent evaluating their compatibility, and learned what would and would not work. Women his age tend to have grandchildren, he observed, and since his children are college-age with no children, this was an issue for him.

"Some women are obsessed with their grandkids, how cute they are, how smart they are," Rick says. "When I date a woman, I want to get to know her, not her grandchildren." Another woman he dated for a few months was twenty-two years younger than Rick with two small children, a "complicating" factor that led friends to advise him, "You'll never be number one."

Rather than a complication, dating a woman with children was an attraction for Tom K., whose wife died when his sons were four and nine. By the time he met Sheila, now his wife, the boys were six and eleven. At first "things were rocky" between Sheila and Nick, the older son, but now that Nick is twenty-eight, they have a good friendship.

As a mother of three children of her own, Sheila helped six-year-old Ben through some health issues that had plagued him after his premature birth. After ten years of helping her first husband through cancer, Sheila was aggressive about seeking medical attention for Ben, who needed to put weight on. She knew that adding liquid nutritional supplements to his diet would help him do so. She also encouraged doctors to check his thyroid "because he just wasn't growing."

"Although Ben remembers his birth mother, he considers Sheila his mom," says Tom. Clearly, dating someone with children and blending families was the right decision for Tom and Sheila.

Since older widows and widowers rarely have small children to care for, dating fulfills needs other than finding a soul mate with whom to raise a family.

Researchers Kris Bulcroft and Margaret O'Connor wanted to see how important dating was to the well-being of older persons. What they found in their research is that dating is clearly a "hedge against loneliness," according to their 1986 article in *Family Relations*. Dating may provide older couples with someone who is a friend, lover, emotional confidant, and caregiver. Although the "companion" role is valued more highly that the "lover" role, it is an unfounded stereotype that older persons are not sexually active in a dating relationship.[49]

What Are the Risks?

Sex outside of marriage at any age, especially with multiple partners, is not without risks. Kirsten Smith and Nicholas Christakis wanted to find out whether widowhood is associated with increased sexual risk-taking, a question of particular concern because untreated sexually transmitted infections (STIs) can lead to other infections, including HIV. In a 2009 article in *Research and Practice*, the authors cited some statistics about multiple sexual partners in this age group: one national study "found that 5.5% of Americans aged 50 to 75 years reported having engaged in sexual behaviors identified as HIV risk factors, including 2.2% with multiple partnerships in the previous year." And many did not use condoms.

What they concluded was that widowhood increased the risk of STIs for men but not for women, which is understandable since older men show "higher levels of sexual desire, greater sexual frequency, and more sexual partners" than older women. And older men remain sexually active longer these days with the introduction of prescriptions to treat erectile dysfunction (ED).

When Pfizer introduced sildenafil (Viagra) with a huge media campaign, "it set a record for having the fastest initial sales growth of any pharmaceutical," according to the article. With the introduction of pills to treat ED, many writers in the popular press worried about an epidemic of STIs, including HIV, among older people. Although the predictions have not come true, Smith and Christakis's study makes a modest claim based on a small sample "that the elevated risk of STI diagnosis associated with widowhood for men appeared to have increased after the introduction of sildenafil."[50]

The researchers note that few physicians talk to patients over fifty about the risk of infection related to sexual activity, though many patients would like them to raise the topic. Since sexually active older widowers are at increased risk for STIs, especially if they are on medicine for erectile dysfunction, they may have to be the first to speak up during an annual physical, no matter how awkward it may be.

If you date again after the death of your spouse, the decision to become sexually active or not is an important one as the new relationship progresses. After four months, Jane cut off a relationship "because of the whole physical thing. He wanted sexual relations, and I didn't feel it was right for us," she says. "When it's right in a relationship, you know it, because it's a beautiful thing."

The sexual urge can be strong in both men and women. A friend who facilitates a grief group recalls overhearing some women talking about missing the sexual part of their marriage, one joking, "Heck, I'd just be happy for a good one-night stand."

In addition to health risks, sexual engagement while dating can complicate a relationship, especially if both partners find sex mutually satisfying. If other parts of dating are not going so well, the pull of sexual intimacy can sometimes make it more difficult to assess the quality of other crucial aspects of the relationship.

Dating is not for every widow or widower. Even if you take the leap into this new social realm, you may be hesitant to give up some of the other pluses of being single, like a rich pool of friends, a satisfying job, and independence. And you could open yourself to hurt.

The only man I ever dated after Scott's death seemed like a wonderful match for my interests and values. He brought a sense of fun and intellectual challenge to my life. After a year and a half, thinking the relationship was stuck, I asked him whether he felt capable of a deeper emotional and time commitment to me, though I was not ready for marriage. After several days of considering my question, he decided he couldn't make that commitment at that time, so we stopped seeing each other.

It was another grief experience, not like "the big one," Scott's death, but a blow. Six years after the break-up, when I thought I was "over it," I visited an acupuncturist for help with anxiety I was experiencing after a traumatizing auto accident. I was lying on the table, doing what the doctor had asked me to do, visualizing the accident and any other unexpected "violence," even unintentional, like the time I tripped over a rock and split open my lip one night while walking the dog. Tears started streaming down my cheeks as I remembered walking in the park with the second man I had fallen in love with only to hear the relationship was over. Like the red-light-running SUV that had taken me by surprise and totaled my car, his decision had blindsided me and done more emotional damage than I had ever admitted.

Several times over the eight years after the break-up, he asked if we could talk, but two times I refused, knowing that I could not allow myself to be hurt again. The third time he asked, I met him to talk over breakfast. After two hours of open conversation about his earlier decision, I agreed to see him, but only a few times until I could assess whether I was ready to pick up where we had left off.

What I told him was this: "I am as happy as I have ever been since Scott died. I have three incredible daughters, their husbands, my grandchildren, my family and friends, a job I love. My life is very full and I feel physically, spiritually, and emotionally balanced. The key will be, does our relationship destroy this balance, or does it make me happier?"

Right now, you may be aching for a sense of balance and fulfillment. It takes a while. Take your pulse occasionally—Are you happy? Who helps you fill the void of a confidant in your life? Are your intimacy needs being fulfilled, even if not through dating? Do you see your life coming back into balance, and, if not, what will make that happen?

Over her eight years of dating Jane has made a habit of keeping in touch with her feelings and her needs. Her bottom line is worth remembering: "No matter what happens, I am committed to making sure I'm true to myself and living out my values"— a pretty good formula for happiness for any widowed person moving toward healing.

Reflection Points

• If you are participating in a grief group, have the courage to ask others how they have dealt with the loss of their spouse-confidant. Who fills that role of confidant in their lives now? How do they cope with the loss of intimacy, especially touch, in their lives?

• If you have started dating seriously, be sure to keep your children, even grown ones, in the loop. Plan a meal with the new man or woman in your life so all your children, their spouses, and your grandchildren can get to know this someone who has become an important part of your life.

Role Model: Wally Bookser

Widowed at age seventy-eight after a near-perfect marriage to Kit, his wife of fifty-six years, Wally lived alone for two years, then sold the family home and moved to another city to be close to four of his six daughters. Because he felt physically and emotionally "rocky" after several intense years of caring for Kit at home, he moved into an assisted-living facility, but longed for companionship of more active seniors.

It was at a senior dance group that he met Vera, at first a casual companion, now his second soul mate, who renewed his zest for life. Consulting lawyers about financial ramifications for both in marrying, they agreed to being permanently engaged. Wally maintains a separate residence, but he admits, "I spend lots of time at Vera's." When they look back on the evolution of their relationship, they believe their meeting was providential. "Our first dance was near Kit's and my wedding anniversary," he says, adding, "Do you think she had something to do with bringing us together?"

Prayer

Loving God, you inspired poetic writers to pen words about intense human love, like these from the Song of Solomon: "Ah, you are beautiful, my beloved, truly lovely" (1:16). When I ache for my spouse's hugs, kisses, or special caresses, help me not only to embrace my sadness but to acknowledge with gratitude these sacred gifts that were part of my married life. Touch me with your grace as I move through this physical and emotional void in my life.

CHAPTER EIGHT

Engaging Your Passions, Renewing Your Joy

We often ask, "What's wrong?" Doing so, we invite painful seeds of sorrow to come up and manifest. We feel suffering, anger, and depression, and produce more such seeds. We would be much happier if we tried to stay in touch with the healthy, joyful seeds inside us and around us. We should learn to ask, "What's not wrong?" and be in touch with that.[51]

—Thich Nhat Hanh

THIS MUCH I know: I would never have made it through Scott's illness without my sisters and friends. Here's what I also know: I would never have survived the years after his death without those same people reminding me to distill as much joy as possible from what could have turned into a totally wretched time in my life.

I have always been an upbeat person; even the clerks at one local convenience store referred to me not by name but as "that happy lady." Would the widowhood experience, often involving a reexamination of self or identity transformation, change the essential me? Those who loved me vowed not to let that happen.

One memory from when Scott was recovering from brain surgery still remains vibrant, only because of the delighted response I got from a friend when I shared it with her. I had been walking with Scott down our street, a slow walk since he was using a cane to steady himself, when I noted colorful words freshly painted on the drainage sewers. They turned out to be warnings from a local environmental group worried that motor oils and contaminated water were being dumped into the sewers. "Drains to the river" was the message. With Scott's cancer always on my mind, I read the words as "Brains to the river."

"That is so wonderful!" laughed my wise friend. "You have to start writing some of these things down so you don't forget them." I didn't write them down but I didn't forget. She had transformed my fear-distorted reading into something to revel in, word play, just my forte.

In my first week back to teaching after Scott's summer surgery, another friend, concerned that I looked exhausted, moved her cozy stuffed chair down the hall to my office so I could nap at will on campus. She also found time in her busy schedule to comfort and engage me with her empathetic listening skills. During one conversation, she told me something I will never forget: "These are hard times for you. What you and your girls are going through is awful. But you must try your best to stay in touch with your playful inner self." A few weeks later she presented me with a birthday gift, a small pewter pin depicting a half-dozen acrobats tumbling over one another in a playful frolic.

Ask most people looking in at widowhood from their uninitiated vantage point what words come to mind. Probably *sad, tragic, depressed, terrible.* But those on the inside of the circle of surviving spouses may suggest a few more: *optimistic, joyful, grateful,* to name a few. Despite the blow the death of a spouse deals to them, many widowed persons see this turning point in their lives as an opportunity to dig deeply into their inner resources, to explore latent talents and passions, and to embrace an optimistic stance toward the remainder of their transformed lives.

Olympia J. Snowe, retired senator from Maine, is a good example. In a 2012 column in the *New York Times*, she shares the attitude that began to define her life when she was orphaned at age ten: "I realized early on that I had a choice: allow myself to become overwhelmed by tragedies or learn something from them. And thankfully, as I was surrounded by the twin strengths of family and faith, I was positioned to view any setbacks as temporary, not permanent."

Sixteen years later, that resolution would be challenged when her husband, a member of the Maine House of Representatives, died in a car accident. Even in her immediate grief, friends were urging her to leverage her college degree in political science and her work with government agencies to run for her husband's vacated seat. She ran, and she won.

"Little could I have known that a forty-year-journey in elective office would commence just four years after my graduation, with a horrific event that could have been the end for me, rather than a beginning," she writes. "I would never have wanted to face a crucial career choice at that perilous personal juncture, but it reminded me once again that it is possible to distill triumph from adversity. Because it's not a question of whether you will encounter difficulties in life; it's really a question of how you confront them."[52]

Many widowed persons show similar resilience as they move on after their spouse's death. In a 2004 study published in *Ageing International*, psychologist Norm O'Rourke examined 232 widows over eighteen months to discover what in their lives contributed to their well-being. The factor that emerged most clearly was "commitment to living." He concluded that the women "seem to have reconciled themselves to their loss; widowhood does not appear to define their existence, but stands as (a) significant life event from which they have moved on." The key in the case of these women: "a positive future orientation."[53]

There are other traits that define the resilient widows and widowers I know. Psychiatrist Frederic Flach lists some of these inner strengths in his book *Resilience: Discovering a New Strength at Times of Stress*:

- a strong, supple sense of self-esteem
- a high level of personal discipline and a sense of responsibility
- recognition and development of one's special gifts and talents
- creativity: open-mindedness, receptivity to new ideas, willingness to dream
- a wide range of interests
- a keen sense of humor
- high tolerance for distress, but not too high
- focus and a commitment to life
- faith, a philosophical and spiritual framework within which personal experiences can be interpreted and understood with meaning and hope, even at life's seemingly most hopeless moments.[54]

Not long after her husband, Mike, died from stage four colon cancer, Beth used her artistic talents not only to express her grief but also to honor her husband's life. In an artist's statement hung next to her painting "Mike's Birch," she describes her process in capturing the back-yard tree under which Mike's ashes had been strewn: sitting under the tree at sunrise, sliding the color wheel to capture the right hues, dividing shapes into "highlights, medium tones, and shades."

She goes on: "The result is a moving tribute of my husband's ashes reaching into the ivy below, down to protect the roots of the tree as his remains become the very bed upon which the tree roots, the tree's lifelines, rely."

Reflecting on her months of grief and her efforts to move on, she concludes: "My own life is built upon the foundations of Mike's love, with whom I share two talented sons. The past two years have been those of caregiving, mothering, and grieving. A year out and I begin to look forward to who I am after 'us,' and how I will design the rest of my life."

Like Beth, Sherrin is an artist, but a verbal one. She had always worked in careers that required writing, but it was technical writing, mostly strategic plans and grant proposals. During her husband Ray's illness, she managed to find time for creative essay writing by partici- pating in a women's writing group in her village. The group, which had been founded in 1877 and met twice a month from autumn through spring, was a reflective outlet for Sherrin.

During Ray's illness writing was a problem, Sherrin says, because it was difficult to concentrate. She had never been a caregiver or a mother, so she was unsure about the how-tos of her new role as companion to Ray in his fight with cancer. She discovered a role model in Mother Teresa, whose life and words filled pages of periodicals and books, espe- cially after her recent death.

"Everything she wrote was short, probably because she was so busy caring for others," says Sherrin. "As a caregiver myself, I had to change my style of writing. I jotted down short thoughts—like Mother Teresa— that I could pull together later." Her favorite writing spot was the corner of the sofa, where she and her husband in the next room could keep an eye on one another, "so he wouldn't feel alone."

Soon after his death she realized that she had been assigned as one of two writers to share pieces with the group in the first meeting in the fall. Distracted and unfocused as she walked home from the market one day, she "was practically in tears. I stopped at our small library and found a friendly librarian who suggested topics for the essay I had to write. I settled on writing about porches. I needed a comfortable topic because of where I was in my grief."

Like other women in the group, before sharing with others Sherrin had regularly practiced reading her pieces aloud to her husband, who would give feedback about content and delivery. This time, she had to go it alone. "Finishing 'The American Porch' essay was a big accomplishment," she remembers. "I had a feeling it would be well received."

In the essay she writes, "So many good things happened on our family porches." She was able to remember her own house, with a sweeping porch that allowed family and friends to move comfortably in and out of groups and conversations. The piece took her back to a time and place "where so many happy things happened, simple things in my life."

Writing is not therapy for Sherrin, but continues to be an essential part of her life as a widow. "My writing group was and still is important to me," she says. "Writing that paper on porches didn't heal me, but if I had not gone back to the group after Ray's death, I would not be as far along in the healing process as I am."

Follow Your Bliss (Gingerly, If Necessary)

Discovering new passions and new life after a spouse's death can come as a surprise to the widowed, as it did for Evelyn Greenslade, a character in Deborah Moggach's novel *The Best Exotic Marigold Hotel*. After a long, dependent relationship with her husband, Hugh, Evelyn finds herself adrift in an unfamiliar, isolated world where she does not know how to use a computer, where phone help comes from technical support in India, where her formerly narrow life in Sussex, England, is exploding as the city experiences the effects of globalization.

Growing increasing fearful in her old age, she surprises herself by moving to a retirement home in India named The Best Exotic Marigold Hotel. Talking about moving to India with the caregiver at her retirement home in the UK, she finds herself invigorated with the possibilities in India; the very name of the country "sharpened her senses, like squeezed lemon." Once settled into the hotel there, "for the first time Evelyn felt it might be possible to make a life for herself here, with her new friends."[55]

In the film version of the novel, also titled *The Best Exotic Marigold Hotel*, Evelyn enters the workforce for the first time in her life, instructing the young tech support staff at a call center in India about the traditions and language quirks of the British callers on the other end of the line. Near the end of the film, we rejoice that Evelyn has not only figured out how to use a laptop and e-mail, but has begun sharing her new experiences on her daily blog.

My own personal transformation during widowhood was more physical than intellectual and professional. But like Evelyn, it forced me out of my comfortable routines and into an environment where I had to take risks.

It all started casually, when the wife of a colleague told me she had once been a principal dancer in the national ballet company of Panama. The conversation conjured up memories of several teenage years of ballet and jazz at my hometown YWCA with Miss Thompson, an aging ballerina. I had loved the costumes (I can still visualize my long-sleeved turquoise leotard with sequins running down the arms), the pointe shoes, the music, but mostly the ecstasy of gliding and whirling across the worn wood floor at the old Y.

Even with my friend's personal invitation to join an adult "beginner" ballet class where she would be substitute teacher in a few months, I hesitated. First, the cost—of lessons and appropriate clothes—but more, the embarrassment at my body revealed in all its flaws in ballet clothes. To every objection, she had a comeback.

"I'll let you have a sixteen-class pass I bought. It still has some lessons left on it."

"Just wear a T-shirt, warm-up pants, and socks. No need to buy anything special until you see if you like it."

I had weighed her invitation all summer, and was about to dismiss the notion of ballet at my age as silly, when she e-mailed me, reminding me of the nights she would be teaching, urging me to come.

So, here I was, in a mirror-lined studio, from which lithe young girls had just come streaming out a few minutes earlier. Looking around, I saw women my age, and some younger, all in leotards, tights, and sheer, short wraps covering their stomachs and hips. I began to waver, but it was too late to back out.

The barre exercises humiliated me. The French words bewildered me, sounding more like cooking terms than dance terms. I didn't know a fondue from a frappé, so I kept stealing glances at the others, who seemed confident and relaxed; they were enjoying themselves. Out on the floor after warm-ups, I felt more like a gangly baby giraffe, legs and feet splaying at wrong angles, than the prima ballerina I had imagined myself in my youth. The ninety minutes dragged on interminably.

"You did great. It gets better each time," my teacher smiled as she hugged me. "Come back on Thursday." And I did. Not only because of her encouragement but because my daughters, sisters, and friends all urged me on. For my sixtieth birthday, I bought black ballet shoes and a pass for more sessions.

I rarely miss a Saturday of ballet now. The ninety minutes provide a time to focus, to relieve myself of outside concerns, to fall into the rhythms of predictable routines, to revel in the beauty of music and movement.

And, it's just plain fun. After a few years of classes with a retired ballerina, our class was a bit nervous when we heard our new instructor would be a principal dancer with the Cincinnati Ballet. Would we measure up? At first we were hesitant, as was she, but we have bonded into a group that keep track of each others' travels and illnesses, who cheer others on as we gingerly attempt floor exercises of arabesques and tour jetés, and laugh heartily as our instructor, with a playful grin, pronounces our efforts as "well, maybe a B-."

Having fun in widowhood is not a contradiction or a sacrilege; it's essential. As early as 1976, physician Norman Cousins recounted in *Anatomy of an Illness* the healing effect humor had on his own health. Since that time, researchers and health professionals have confirmed his experience through numerous studies. In his 1989 book *Head First: The Biology of Hope*, Cousins recalls the skepticism that greeted his first book. Now, he writes,

> Perhaps I might have been a lot less defensive if I had known then what I know now. Medical researchers at a dozen or more medical centers have been probing the effects of laughter on the human body and have detailed a wide array of beneficial changes—all the way from enhanced respiration to increases in the number of disease-fighting immune cells. Extensive experiments have been conducted, working with a significant number of human beings, showing that laughter contributes to good health. Scientific evidence is accumulating to support the biblical axiom that "a merry heart doeth good like a medicine."[56]

For a 2008 article, "Humor, Laughter, and Happiness in the Daily Lives of Recently Bereaved Spouses," sociologist Dale Lund and associates examined 292 recently widowed men and women. The researchers concluded that "most of the bereaved spouses rated humor and happiness as being very important in their daily lives and that they were also experiencing these emotions at higher levels than expected." The degree to which they reported happy emotions surprised Lund because the widowed persons were interviewed between five and twenty-four weeks after the deaths of their spouses.

Opportunities to experience humor and laughter threaded through their lives in significant ways, according to responses to these prompts:

During the past week …
- I have enjoyed the humor of others, 76.6%
- I had a good laugh at something, 75.3%
- I did something that made me feel happy, 85.5%
- Someone else did something that made me feel happy, 88.6%
- I felt happy about something, 89.6%[57]

As Norman Cousins points out,

It is a serious error to suppose that laughter is the only emotional antidote to stress or illness…. An appreciation of life can be a prime tonic for mind and body. Being able to respond to the majesty of the way nature fashions its art…the purring of a kitten perched on your shoulder, or the head of a dog snuggling under your hand; the measured power of Beethoven's *Emperor* Concerto, the joyous quality of a Chopin nocturne… the sound of delight in a young boy's voice in catching his first baseball, and, most of all, the expression in the face of someone who loves you—all these are but a small part of a list of wondrous satisfactions that come with the gift of awareness and that nourish even as they heal.[58]

As you move through the widow events of your life, despite the overwhelming sadness that blankets your world, be open to the people and situations that allow you to feel new and alive, that bring you joy in the midst of daily crises, that startle you into a fresh appreciation of the wonder of life.

Like the fictional widow Evelyn Greenslade, let go of your fear and embrace new experiences that present themselves. When she ventured from the comfort of her room in the Marigold Hotel into the neighborhood beyond, she found that "the street outside teemed with life." Her new city was ripe with life-giving surprises. In the movie, Evelyn tells her friend Muriel, "Nothing here has worked out quite as I expected," to which Muriel replies, "Most things don't. But sometimes what happens instead is the good stuff."

Reflection Points

• Ask a friend to watch a funny movie with you, either at home or in a theater. Allow yourself to laugh out loud at the funny parts, and to rehash those parts when the movie is over.

• Check the weather forecast for clear skies in the next few days, then mark your calendar for quiet time at dawn or sunset. Revel in the gifts of light, color, and tranquility your experience showers on you.

Role Model: Kathy Braswell

After Kathy's husband, Jack, retired they moved to a home on a golf course in North Carolina, socializing often with neighbors and leading "an idyllic life." With Jack's diagnosis of colon cancer, life changed dramatically. "We couldn't do parties anymore. We just weren't interested," she says. They spent much of their time traveling to and from hospitals for treatment.

When a doctor told them that they had run out of treatment options, advising "live every day to the fullest," they hit the ground running. Jack had already visited forty-nine states, so they booked a cruise to Alaska, making adjustments during the trip as his energy peaked or waned. Always, says Kathy, he was upbeat and generous. A few weeks before his death, Kathy found him folding clothes in the basement to be donated to Goodwill after his death. The night before he died, with the little energy he had left, he pulled himself up from his chair, hardly able to walk, and asked her to dance with him.

During Jack's illness, Kathy's friends marveled at her devotion in caring for him. "That's why we're here—to take care of one another," she says. As a widow, Kathy continues to "care for" Jack's life by leading a full life herself in her home near their adult children. "I have made it my purpose to remember the good things about our life together and how fortunate we were," she says. "I try to copy Jack's example of being positive." She is hesitant to offer advice to the newly widowed, saying, "It's a different trip for everybody. We each have to figure it out for ourselves."

Prayer

Joyful God of creation, you said, "Let there be light," and there was light. You saw that the light was good, and you separated the light from the darkness. Help me to find glimmers of joy and happiness in my life as I work to pull myself out of my darkness. Let me be open to the places, events, and people that bring a smile to my face and a hearty laugh to my lips.

CHAPTER NINE

Outward Bound

For over a decade, I've followed the travels of a former student who has led an adventuresome life as a staff member of Outward Bound, an international education program. He describes the program's mission as "taking people outside their comfort zones into inspiring, challenging and unknown environments where they can grow."

Having worked in the Florida Everglades, the snowy terrain of Montana, and a camp nestled in hills outside Mexico City, Patrick recently signed on with Outward Bound in Hong Kong. When he was in town on his way to Hong Kong, we caught up on his work and his life. Our conversation supplied an image that strikes me as relevant to widows and widowers trying to move forward on their healing journeys. "Outward bound," Patrick explained, is a nautical term to describe "a ship leaving the harbor. A ship is safe in harbor but was never built to stay in harbor."

None of us who has lost a spouse can predict when we will be ready to move out of safe harbors beyond our comfort zones into open waters. But it must happen, if we are to thrive. That moment may sneak up on you, unexpectedly, as it did with Sherrin. She remembers about eighteen months after her husband's death that "I was happier than I had been in a long time and knew I had turned some psychological corner." Pinpointing that shift may be difficult, but it usually means moving into a place of peace about death.

Nineteenth-century Americans followed a carefully prescribed set of customs after a family member's death. Survivors knew how long they should mourn, what they should wear, when they could venture out of the house or accept visitors. Although contemporary widows and widowers have more leeway in dress and behavior than their predecessors, in some ways our approach to death is less satisfying, more bewildering. In the nineteenth century death was a fact of life; in today's culture it is a mystery to be feared.

As a student of American literature, I am well-acquainted with poetry, fiction, and narratives that describe anxious wives on the New England coast pacing the railed roofs of their homes awaiting the arrival of seafaring husbands a year or more after they had set sail on a whaler or trading ship. Where the women paced was aptly named a "widow's walk," since the news about the fate of their husbands' vessels was often grim.

Back then, however, both men and women knew how to deal with death. Men often married two or three times as each successive wife died in childbirth. For Emily Dickinson death was so real that it is a recurring theme in her poetry. After his brother was hospitalized during the Civil War, Walt Whitman made a ministry of visiting wounded and dying Union soldiers in military hospitals outside the nation's capital. Each day, he would dress in white, groom his flowing beard, and venture among the dying soldiers to pen farewell letters to wives or mothers, and hold the soldiers' hands as they lay dying.

Such acceptance of death is rare in most twenty-first–century Western societies. Death, says Janet McCord, a scholar who specializes in death, dying, grief, and bereavement, has become the "d-word," one rarely uttered by relatives or members of the medical profession.

Accepting Death as Normal

Why the shift in attitudes toward death? One factor, McCord says, is a "medical culture that believes that if a patient dies, members of that profession have failed. Medicine tells us, and we believe it, that death is optional. We always think there is more we can do to stay alive. But death is normal and will happen to all of us."

As surviving spouses, we already know that. We also have come to accept that circumstances of life and death are often beyond our control. Because we have dealt with death, we have much to offer should we choose to use the wisdom gleaned from our experience to shepherd the newly widowed through the first frightening steps on their journey to wholeness.

Outreach is simple, and relatively cheap. Send a card, with the briefest of notes, to new widows and widowers. E-mail? It's certainly an option if that's a means of communication you feel most comfortable with. But there are so many simple and varied cards, often priced at under a dollar, that the cost of a card plus postage makes the choice clear to me. A card is something physical to hold, savor, and offer comfort, over and over again.

When you feel emotionally strong enough, attending wakes or funerals is a powerful statement of solidarity with the newest members of a "club" no one wants to join. It took a while after Scott's death before I could handle the emotions of a funeral. I had planned to attend one at my parish for the young daughter of a couple who often sat near me in church. I made it to the church parking lot, but when I started to cry in my car I resigned myself to sending a note of support.

I clearly remember my first "successful" funeral after Scott's death: it was for the father of a colleague who was also my former student. I willed myself through the Mass, grateful that it was her father, and not her husband.

One of my favorite segments of National Public Radio's series *This I Believe* was written by Deirdre Sullivan, a New York attorney. She recounts how her father taught her "always go to the funeral. Do it for the family." He pushed her to go solo to a visitation for her fifth-grade teacher. By the time she was sixteen, unlike her classmates, she had been to a half-dozen funerals. But she had no idea how meaningful those visits had been to the bereaved until her own father died. She says,

> On a cold April night three years ago, my father died a quiet death from cancer. His funeral was on a Wednesday, middle of the workweek. I had been numb for days when, for some reason, during the funeral, I turned and looked back at the folks in the church. The memory of it still takes my breath away. The most human, powerful, and humbling thing I've ever seen was a church at 3:00 on a Wednesday full of inconvenienced people who believe in going to the funeral.[59]

My oldest sister describes me to others as a "valiant woman," after the woman described in Proverbs 31. That biblical woman has many qualities that define the men and women who muster up the courage to move on after the devastating loss of a soul mate:

> Strength and dignity are her clothing,
>   and she laughs at the time to come.
> She opens her mouth with wisdom,
>   and the teaching of kindness is on her tongue.
>   —Proverbs 31:25–26

After the wrenching experience you have endured, and the months or years of trying to reorient your life, you may not believe that strength, dignity, laughter, wisdom, and kindness define you. But from the perspective of the newly widowed, you embody those characteristics and hold out hope for their healing.

I know. On my campus and in my parish, after a man or woman loses a spouse, what I hear is "I know you will be there for them." I never intrude on anyone's grief, but I let them know that I am there to listen, support, walk with them—however limited that role may be.

For a while after Scott's death, I felt drawn to the quiet waters of comforting people and places, where I was securely anchored, unbuffetted by winds or waves. But at some point, I knew I was ready to venture forth and begin reclaiming my life. Wanting once again to feel fully alive, to share with others the graces of my widow's journey, I accepted the challenge of hoisting my sails, waiting for the right wind, then heading "outward bound." At first, it was a choppy ride, but overall it has been exhilarating. In Patrick's words, I have moved outside my "comfort zone" into an "unknown environment," life after death. Like his Outward Bound trips, my new adventure has been both inspiring and challenging.

Moving out of that harbor can be frightening, because it's uncharted territory. But for most widows and widowers, it's a decision that leads to growth in ways and degrees they could never have predicted.

In the introductory invitation in this book, the journey of widowhood was described as one filled with choices to be made on the path to wholeness and healing after the death of a spouse. An apt motto for the journey that lies ahead as you finish this book and move on is a simple one, a favorite exhortation of mine from the book of Deuteronomy (30:19): "Choose life."

1. Elizabeth Bayley Seton, *Collected Writings, Volume I* (Hyde Park, N.Y.: New City, 2000), p. 275.

2. Alice Parsons Zulli, "Healing Rituals: Powerful and Empowering," www.hospicefoundation.org.

3. C.S. Lewis, *A Grief Observed* (New York: Seabury, 1961), pp. 47, 9.

4. Walter Brueggemann, *Praying the Psalms* (Winona, Minn.: Saint Mary's, 1993), pp. 13–14, 19.

5. Emily Dickinson, *The Complete Poems of Emily Dickinson,* Thomas H. Johnson, ed. (Cambridge, Mass.: Harvard University Press, 1961), p. 460.

6. Brueggemann, p. 25.

7. Richard Groves, *Sacred Art of Living Spiritual Foundation,* www.sacredartofliving.org.

8. Elisabeth Kübler-Ross, *Elisabeth Kübler-Ross Foundation,* www.ekrfoundation.org.

9. Seton, p. 275.

10. Dickinson, p. 497.

11. Jane Burgess Kohn and Willard K. Kohn, *The Widower* (Boston: Beacon, 1978), pp. 69, 76, 77.

12. Social Security Administration, http://www.ssa.gov/survivorplan/index.htm.

13. Dag Hammarskjöld, *Markings,* Leif Sjöberg and W.H. Auden, trans. (New York: Alfred A. Knopf, 1964), p. 62.

14. Harvey G. Cox, *On Not Leaving It to the Snake* (New York: Macmillan, 1964), p. viii.

15. Tamara Ferguson, in Irwin Gerber et al., eds., *Perspectives on Bereavement* (New York: Arno, 1979), p. 35.

16. *Spousal Bereavement in Late Life,* Carr, et al., eds. (New York: Springer, 2006), p. 173.

17. *Spousal Bereavement in Late Life,* p. 179.

18. "Your Road to Confidence: A Widow's Guide to Buying, Selling and Maintaining a Car" (Hartford, Conn.: The Hartford Financial Services Group, 2011), p. 2.

19. "Your Road to Confidence," p. 17.

20. "Your Road to Confidence," p. 7.

21. The Cohousing Association of the United States, http://www.cohousing.org/what_is_cohousing.

22. The Older Women's Co-Housing Group, http://www.owch.org.uk/owchpages/history.html.

23. Mary Beth Franklin, The Kiplinger, 2009, www.kiplinger.com.

24. Harriet Beecher Stowe, quoted in Dorie McCullough Lawson, *Posterity: Letters of Great Americans to Their Children* (New York: Doubleday, 2004), pp. 228–229.

25. "A Guide for the Newly Widowed," at www.aarp.org/relationships/grief-loss/info-2005/newly_widowed.html.

26. Bragi Skulason et al., "Assessing Survival in Widowers, and Controls—A Nationwide, Six-to-Nine-Year Follow-Up," *BMC Public Health,* 2012, p. 96.

27. Eran Shor et al., "Widowhood and Mortality: A Meta-Analysis and Meta-Regression," *Demography,* 2012, p. 598.

28. *Spousal Bereavement in Late Life,* p. 132.

29. János Pilling et al., "Alcohol use in the first three years of bereavement: a national representative survey," *Substance Abuse Treatment, Prevention, and Policy,* 2012, p. 4.

30. Reynolds, quoted in Tara Parker-Pope, "The Surprising Shortcut to Better Health," http://well.blogs.nytimes.com/2012/05/04/the-surprising-shortcut-to-better-health/.

31. M. Katherine Shear et al., "Review: Complicated Grief and Related Bereavement Issues for DSM-5," *Depression and Anxiety,* 2011, p. 108.

32. "What Can I Do About My Grief?" *Hamilton's Academy of Grief and Loss,* www.HamiltonsFuneralHome.com.

33. Susan Nolen-Hoeksema and Judith Larson, *Coping with Loss* (Mahwah, N.J.: Lawrence Erlbaum, 1999), p. 15.

34. Neil Chethik, *Father Loss: How Sons of All Ages Come to Terms with the Deaths of Their Dads* (New York: Hyperion, 2001), pp. 6, 154, 158, 162, 164.

35. Helena Znaniecka Lopata, "Contributions of Extended Families to the Support Systems of Metropolitan Area Widows: Limitations of the Modified Kin Network," *Journal of Marriage and the Family,* May 1978, pp. 355–364.

36. Colin Murray Parkes and Robert S. Weiss, *Recovery from Bereavement* (New York: Basic, 1983), p. 163.

37. André Toth and Susan Toth, "Group Work with Widowers." *Social Work,* January 1980, pp. 63–64.

38. Therese A. Rando, *How to Go on Living When Someone You Love Dies* (New York: Bantam, 1991), p. 311.

39. Ruth Davis Konigsberg, "5 Surprising Truths About Grief," available at http://www.aarp.org/relationships/grief-loss/info-03-2011/truth-about-grief.2.html.

40. E. Annie Proulx, *The Shipping News* (New York: Scribner, 1993), pp. 331–332.

41. J. William Worden, *Children and Grief: When a Parent Dies* (New York: Guilford, 1996), pp. 9, 13.

42. Joe Biden, *Promises to Keep: On Life and Politics* (New York: Random House, 2008), pp. xxii.

43. Marge Piercy, "The Tao of Touch," *The Hunger Moon: New and Selected Poems, 1980–2010* (New York: Alfred A. Knopf, 2011), p. 318.

44. Jung-Hwa Ha, "Changes in Support from Confidants, Children, and Friends Following Widowhood," *Journal of Marriage and Family,* May 2008, p. 307.

45. Piercy, p. 318.

46. AARP/Modern Maturity, *Sexuality Study* (Atlanta: NFO Research, 1999), p. 13.

47. Deborah Carr, "The Desire to Date and Remarry Among Older Widows and Widowers," *Journal of Marriage and Family,* November 2004, pp. 1051–1068.

48. Maria M. Talbott, "Older widows' attitudes towards men and remarriage," *Journal of Aging Studies,* Winter 98, pp. 429–451.

49. Kris Bulcroft and Margaret O'Connor, "The Importance of Dating Relationships on Quality of Life for Older Persons," *Family Relations,* July 1986, pp. 397–401.

50. Kristen P. Smith and Nicholas A. Christakis, "Association Between Widowhood and Risk of Diagnosis with a Sexually Transmitted Infection in Older Adults," *American Journal of Public Health,* November 2009, pp. 2055–2062.

51. Thich Nhat Hanh, *Peace Is Every Step: The Path of Mindfulness in Everyday Life* (New York: Bantam, 1991), p. 77.

52. Olympia J. Snowe, "My Brilliant Career: Politician," *The New York Times,* June 2, 2012, http://www.nytimes.com/2012/06/03/opinion/sunday/olympia-snowe-03job3.html?_r=0.

53. Norm O'Rourke, "Psychological Resilience and the Well-Being of Widowed Women," *Ageing International,* Summer 2004, pp. 267–280.

54. Frederic Flach, *Resilience: Discovering a New Strength at Times of Stress* (New York: Hatherleigh, 1997), p. 105.

55. Deborah Moggach, *The Best Exotic Marigold Hotel* (New York: Random House, 2004), pp. 52, 135.

56. Norman Cousins, *Head First: The Biology of Hope* (New York: E.P. Dutton, 1989), p. 127.

57. Dale A. Lund et al., "Humor, Laughter, and Happiness in the Daily Lives of Recently Bereaved Spouses," *Omega, Journal of Death and Dying,* 2008–2009, pp. 87, 94.

58. Cousins, pp. 146–147.

59. Deirdre Sullivan, quoted in Jay Allison and Dan Gediman, eds., *This I Believe: The Personal Philosophies of Remarkable Men and Women* (New York: Holt, 2007), p. 237.

ABOUT THE AUTHOR

Elizabeth Bookser Barkley, PH.D., is professor and chair of the department of English and modern languages at the College of Mount St. Joseph in Cincinnati. She is the author of *Handing on the Faith: When You Are a Godparent, Loving the Everyday: Meditations for Moms,* and *Woman to Woman: Seeing God in Everyday Life.*